THE **PHISH** BOOK

THE

PHISH BOOK

RICHARD GEHR
& PHISH

VILLARD
NEW YORK

PRODUCED BY John Paluska and Jason Colton/Dionysian Productions, Burlington, Vermont
BOOK DESIGN: Helene Silverman/Hello Studio
RESEARCH ASSISTANCE: Kevin Shapiro and Bart Stephens
SPECIAL THANKS TO Brian DeFiore, Mollie Doyle, Joanne Barracca,
Beth Pearson, and Janet Wygal at Villard Books, and to Tom Marshall and Sarah Lazin

Library of Congress Cataloging-in-Publication Data
Gehr, Richard.
    The Phish book/Richard Gehr and Phish.
        p. cm.
      ISBN: 0-375-75254-4
      1. Phish (Musical group) 2. Rock musicians—United States—Biography.
    I. Phish (Musical group)   II. Title.
ML421.P565G44 1998
782.42166 092 2—dc21 98-19118 MN
[B]

Random House website address: www.atrandom.com
Phish website address: www.phish.com

Printed in the United States of America on acid-free paper

98765432

First Paperback Edition

"IT IS A JOY TO BE
HIDDEN BUT
DISASTER NOT TO
BE FOUND"
D.W. WINNICOTT

THE UNEXPECTED EXPERIENCE: INTRODUCTION

MY FIRST Phish show was a revelation. Assigned by *New York Newsday* to review the Vermont quartet's April 13, 1994, appearance at New York City's Beacon Theater, I attended the show with virtually no expectations and in return experienced nearly everything I could want from a nineties rock band. Phish made me dance, think, and laugh—often at the same time. Affirmative without being cloying, dark but not potentially homicidal, and a lot of the time just plain odd, Phish seemed like heralds of a secret American musical scene that was being purposely kept underground so as to preserve it from defilement.

OPPOSITE: The Great Went, Limestone, Maine, August 16–17, 1997
BELOW: Trey Anastasio, backstage at Colorado State Fair, Pueblo, Colorado, August 23, 1992

At the time, my musical tastes bent toward the tropical, experimental, improvised, and dancehall-euphoric (not necessarily in that order). So, in retrospect, it is no surprise that the Caribbean lilt of "Lizards," the acid nirvana of "Divided Sky," and the unexpected complexity and ominous vocal improvisations of "You Enjoy Myself" resonated with me. Tapes were accumulated, hard-core Phish fans consulted, and soon I felt like an anthropologist on the verge of discovering an inexplicably overlooked tribe residing in my own backyard. More research was definitely in order, and by the end of the year I had hit the road with Phish on behalf of *Spin* magazine, for whom I wrote a feature article about the band. This unusually enjoyable assignment, during which I came to know the band and its extended family and friends, eventually led to this book.

Phish is a litmus test, a musical mirror of listeners' tastes and prejudices; and if the existential thrill of improvised music doesn't appeal to you, look elsewhere. Attending an isolated Phish show without prior experience of their music is not unlike going to a hockey game without knowing what constitutes an offside infringement or a power play. Their audience knows Phish as a big here-comes-everybody sort of band—a continually evolving quartet that challenges its listeners with a constantly fluctuating mosaic of tunes, moods, styles, and influences. The band seems to reinvent itself almost on a nightly basis depending on such

Mike Gordon plays with one of his high school bands, the Tombstone Blues Band, May 1981.

ineffable variables as time, location, and mood. Within the space of a few shows you can hear the band morph between their various identities as savvy arena rockers, intense starship pilots, vaudeville nostalgists, modest American folkies, boundary-dissolving improvisers, roots-conscious spiritualists, and mind-fucking pranksters.

Slippery and abstract, Phish's sound evades easy characterization. In the fall of 1993, however, lyricist Tom Marshall and the band cowrote the song "Wolfman's Brother" for their fourth album, *Hoist,* which would be released the following spring. The unintentionally self-referential lyrics mention a "smooth atonal sound" that was "like a cross between a hurricane / And a ship that's run aground." For nearly fifteen years the band and their audience have grown and developed outside the pop industry's prevailing winds, creating an excitement generated almost solely by the infinitely rich musical possibilities of the live onstage Moment. "So I might be on a side street," an earlier couplet from "Wolfman's Brother" surmises, "or a stairway to the stars." Phish flourish outside mainstream rock and its so-called alternatives. To call them the most popular cult band in the world would not be an overstatement.

I was fortunate enough to hook up with Phish as they were undergoing a period of serious—if not entirely conscious—artistic soul searching. During the course of 1997, when most of this book was researched, Phish toured both Europe and the United States twice, spent four days jamming spontaneously in Bearsville Studios on two separate occasions, and performed a pair of raucous New Year's Eve shows. The record *Slip Stitch and Pass,* released in October, earned the group some of their best reviews to date. The Great Went in August proved that the Clifford Ball—the previous summer's band-sponsored weekend camp-out and six-set musical feast—far from being a one-shot fluke, could be relocated, expanded, and reconceived as

an even more ambitious event that, with sixty-five thousand people in attendance, still managed to slip under the national media's radar. *The Phish Book* reflects that watershed year, commencing with New Year's Eve 1996 and concluding on the same evening a year later.

While discussing Phish's current events during our interviews, which took place throughout 1997 and into 1998, the quartet dipped freely into both their collective and personal histories in order to shed light on whatever was shaping their evolving musical persona at the time our conversations took place. The band's February 1997 tour of European clubs and small theaters, for example, naturally stirred up memories of their earliest days as a New England club band. A summer San Francisco Bay Area appearance became an occasion for the band to delve into their improv-rock roots. And the conversations we had around their Bearsville recording sessions reflected upon Phish's songwriting process and the conditions under which their various albums were recorded. At its best, improvised music resembles an intimate and honest conversation among equals. So consider *The Phish Book* a studio edit of Phish in real-time conversation. I've also added some thoughts and context along the way, while editing the band's own words for clarity, focus, and rhythm.

A capsule history of the band would go something like this: Guitarists Trey Anastasio and Jeff Holdsworth, drummer Jon Fishman, and bassist Mike Gordon met at the University of Vermont in 1983.

Keyboardist Page McConnell joined the group in the fall of 1985, and Holdsworth split the following spring. Many, many shows were played, and a few records were released as the band progressed from performing at small local gigs and parties to doing a residency at the Burlington bar Nectar's, then moving onward and outward across the United States, steadily attracting more and more fans,

like some psychedelic snowball, until eventually the group was forced to graduate from theaters like the Beacon to the arena circuit they focus on currently. Phish has remained together as long as they have by combining personal commitment with constant artistic change.

In a certain sense, everything you'll read herein is part of a single ongoing conversation the band has been engaged in—both onstage and off— for nearly fifteen years. You don't need to spend a lot of time with the four thirtyish musicians to realize how closely their offstage interaction mirrors the musical personalities their audience discovers every time the group hits the stage. Trey Anastasio is guileless, exuberant, and bursting with ideas. Mike Gordon is low-key yet authoritative and possesses a wonderfully droll sense of the absurd. Jon Fishman is confident, intuitive, and splendidly responsive, with a knack for unexpectedly pulling conversational rabbits out of hats. And Page McConnell is as cerebral and tactfully in-the-moment away from the boards as he is when ensconced in their midst.

But Phish's music isn't created in a vacuum. Lighting director Chris Kuroda and live sound mixer Paul Languedoc are key members of a tightly knit tour crew about whom one rarely hears a discouraging word. The Phish organization is perceived, both within and without, as a shockingly functional unit. Manager John Paluska and his staff at Dionysian Productions have steered the band through the snares and pitfalls of an industry hard-pressed to deal with bands that sell relatively few records in comparison to their sales of

concert tickets. And Phish's audience is like an organic, symbiotic entity unto itself that completes the equation, providing the energy, curiosity, and attention that drives the band.

The Phish Book was written under the influence of the music of a band continually in flux. It also includes a wealth of information distilled from the observations of their crew, their management, and various friends, fans, and family members—especially longtime lyricist Tom Marshall. It's a glimpse into an ever-evolving experience firmly rooted in perseverance, dedication, and risk taking. But it's no replacement for the music, which continually tests the limits of what four improvising rock musicians can do onstage and in the studio. In a certain sense, everything Phish plays is part of a single extended composition. This particular fragment of the musical and cultural kaleidoscope that is Phish begins at the end of 1996, as the band stands on the verge of transforming itself once again.

OPPOSITE, TOP:
Page McConnell,
fifth grade
OPPOSITE, BOTTOM:
On the runway at
Plattsburgh Air
Force Base during
the Clifford Ball,
Plattsburgh, New
York, August 17,
1996
ABOVE: Trey per-
forms in Gilbert
and Sullivan's
Ruddigore,
Princeton Day
School, 1978.

Madison Square Garden,
December 31, 1997

TROPICAL HOT-DOG NIGHT: NEW YEAR'S EVE '96

PHISH MAKE New Year's Eve worth leaving the house for. Traditionally the toughest ticket of the year, the band's New Year's Eve shows have been extravagant festivities since December 31, 1989, when Phish played to a packed house in Boston's World Trade Center Exhibition Hall. Fresh fruit and champagne were served to many of the seventeen hundred audience members who attended this faux formal affair, at which the band—with the exception of drummer Jon Fishman, who opted for a G-string and top hat—sported full tuxedoes.

As the group's popularity swelled, New Year's Eve became an occasion for increasingly elaborate stunts. Having combined music with other media from the beginning, Phish approaches the evening as an opportunity to pull out all the stops, play three sets, and demonstrate how fertile a field for high-concept performance art arena rock can still be. As consumers of the expensive rock spectacle, Phish's members were raised on Pink Floyd's flying pigs, David Bowie's elaborate sets, and Gene Simmons's blood spewing from his made-up mouth. Rock always promises more than loud, electric, blues-derived music: It plays with our premillennial desires for bigger, louder, and faster productions.

No matter how enticing their visual displays, however, Phish always place their music foremost in importance. Apart from the hoopla, Phish also regard their New Year's Eve shows as opportunities to sum up a year in their collective musical life, occasions for both celebration and reflection. And December 31, 1996, was both a summation and a turning point for the band. Certain aspects of the band would be left behind that night. Like a reptile shedding its skin, the quartet would emerge several weeks later wearing a substantially different artistic attitude that would become increasingly evident as 1997 progressed.

In 1992, a year after Phish's first three-set New Year's Eve show, the audience at Northeastern University's Matthews Arena in Boston was presented with flyers describing a "secret language." The crowd was to use the language to beguile those listening to the show's radio simulcast with seemingly random applause, shouts of "Eggplant!" and other audio non

OPPOSITE, TOP: The aquarium set, Bender Arena, Washington, D.C., December 28, 1993 BOTTOM: The band "fabricates time," Madison Square Garden, New York, New York, December 31, 1995. OVERLEAF: Boston Garden, Boston, Massachusetts, December 31, 1994

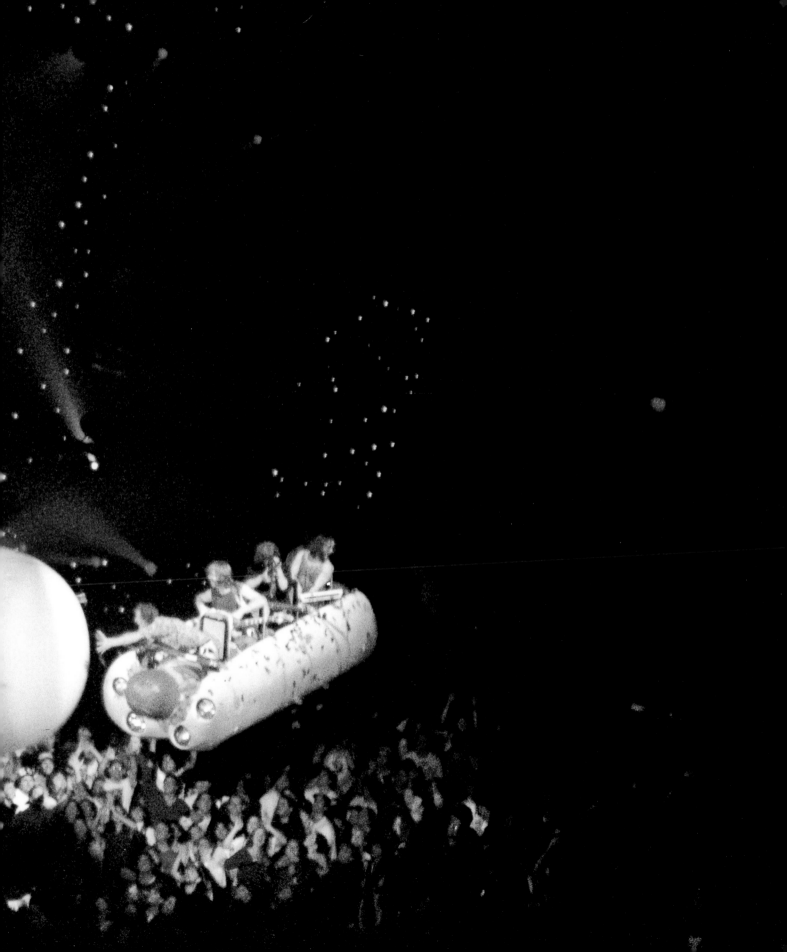

sequiturs. The show's highlights included a rare appearance by musical cohort the Dude of Life, who sang "Diamond Girl" while pushing a lawn mower about the stage.

Phish's first seriously ambitious use of onstage props and theatrics came the following year at the Centrum in Worcester, Massachusetts, where the entire stage was transformed into an immense aquarium. As midnight approached, the still-offstage band could be overheard announcing their desire to go scuba diving. The lights dimmed slowly, and four wet-suited figures descended from the ceiling. A decision (audible to all) was made to investigate the giant clam at the rear of the stage, which opened up as the divers swam into it, then immediately closed, trapping the aquatic quartet. During the ensuing countdown to midnight, the clam levitated above the stage where it shuddered, shook, and erupted into a riot of light and confetti with the band nowhere to be seen. When the dust settled, however, Phish suddenly appeared onstage, still attired in scuba gear, and performed "Auld Lang Syne," having miraculously escaped the sinister bivalve's clutches.

OPPOSITE: Fleet Center, Boston, Massachusetts, December 31, 1996

Phish upped the ante at Boston Garden in 1994. Just before the band's third set, a famished Fishman requested a hot dog, a *huge* hot dog, over the sound system from "backstage." The band returned to the stage, picked up their instruments, and began to play the drummer's bluegrass tune, "My Sweet One." They were soon interrupted, however, by the delivery of a way-oversized hot dog, french fries, and a generic cola beverage that descended to the stage from the rafters on a takeout tray. Putting aside their instruments, the band boarded the hot dog, took off, and flew above the audience to the opposite end of the arena for several minutes while performing "Auld Lang Syne" on portable instruments.

The Madison Square Garden extravaganza the following year was a particularly toothsome show, highlighted by an onstage "time-manufacturing" apparatus complete with Jacob's Ladder, Tesla Coil, and other weird-science appurtenances. During "Colonel Forbin's Ascent," Anastasio explained how the band spent its off-tour months actually "fabricating time" in Gamehendge, the mythical locus of many Phish-related fantasies. Indeed, it behooved the band to produce time this very evening in order to ensure 1996's timely arrival. After all, Anastasio inquired, "What if it remained 1995 forever, and you had to listen to the same song over and over?"—a question answered by lyricist Tom Marshall's lethal rendition of Collective Soul's then-ubiquitous "Shine." A few minutes before twelve, Old Man '96 entered a casket that was hoisted overhead while all four band members stationed themselves at different parts of the time machine. A wild onstage thunderstorm ensued, and at midnight the casket burst open to reveal a freshly shaved and diapered Baby Fishman '97, whose stand-in then sneaked offstage.

Before performing in Boston's then-new Fleet Center on December 31, 1996, Phish had played a long national tour, occasionally performing to half-full arenas in places like Memphis and Kansas City. While they filled arenas in many parts of the country in 1996,

ABOVE: Rehearsing the hot-dog stunt with theatrical designer Chris McGregor (FAR LEFT): Philadelphia Civic Center, Philadelphia, Pennsylvania, December 28, 1994

OPPOSITE: Fleet
Center, December
31, 1996
BELOW: Rehearsing
"Bohemian
Rhapsody" with the
Boston Community
Choir, Fleet
Center, December
31, 1996

Phish still occasionally found themselves in cities that lacked the midsized venues best suited to the band's popularity at the time. It was a period of transition during which both band and management were confronted by the challenge of translating the Phish experience from theaters to arenas while maintaining the intimacy and intensity fans expected. Nineteen ninety-six laid the physical foundation for the radical musical changes the band made the following year. And Chris Kuroda's lights and Paul Languedoc's sound helped ease the transition for audience and musicians alike. "I really enjoy 'human wallpaper' anyway," admits Kuroda, discussing how full houses can become backdrops for his lighting, "and a whole wall of people behind the band looks terrific. It makes even a big room feel cozy."

Having decided they were tired of participating actively in the New Year's Eve theatrics, Phish sought an alternative stunt for New Year's Eve '96, and ultimately chose an exaggerated

version of an old favorite. Thus, at midnight, a potential record deluge of 79,627 balloons floated onto the audience, eventually drowning the band itself as they played a long, raucous "Down with Disease." That was not the night's grand finale, however. They also opted to cover, in their usual meticulous fashion, the most ostentatious hunk of glam rock ever to come down the pike, Queen's "Bohemian Rhapsody," complete with a gospel choir. The ultimate arena-rock gesture, it was also a musically ambitious condensation of the band's traditional Halloween ritual of covering classic rock albums in their entirety.

When I talked to the band members about the fall tour and the Boston New Year's Eve show shortly afterward, they clearly had mixed feelings about the quality of their playing and the venues in which they had performed. While the excitement they felt onstage was undeniable, there was a sense that something important to their further development lay just around the bend. And the fall tour's occasionally rocky road may have been a necessary passage to get them there.

Trey Anastasio: The problem with New Year's Eve is there's too much nervous energy, too many people backstage, too much going on. There's no place to escape except onstage.

Mike Gordon: I loved being immersed in a sea of 79,627 balloons, most of which seemed to wind up on the stage. I sometimes wonder how a little kid would feel coming to his first Phish show. This one would have seemed really big and exciting.

Page McConnell: I was beginning to lose my voice during the show, and it was causing me great distress. This has happened a couple of times during other New Year's runs. I don't know why. But I could hardly talk between sets and was doing everything I could to save my voice for "Bohemian Rhapsody," which has so many high lead parts for me to sing. Other than that, I felt great. I wasn't freaked out because I knew I could pull it off. I glanced at the set list and was happy to see there wouldn't be any major vocal challenges for me until the third set. But I'd never sung "Bohemian Rhapsody" live before. In fact, I hadn't even looked at the music until we got to Philadelphia on December 28, and I spent the next four nights learning it.

Jon "Fish" Fishman: Live music is still the most important thing. It ultimately comes down to something that will tear people away from television, Great Communicator or the Great Deceiver or whatever it is. The thing about live music is it's just so real. It's in the moment. It's human.

Page: Our jamming and playing have improved over the years as we've gotten to know one another better. I usually have peak experiences once or twice a night, although there's the exceptional night when all four of us will think we played very well for an entire set. It's all relative, of course. Not hooking up for us still means hooking up more than most bands do.

Fleet Center,
December 31, 1996

Trey: The stage is absolutely the safest place in my life. I have anti–stage fright apparently, and feel happier and more secure there than anywhere else in the world. It's weird and selfish, but when I'm onstage nobody can bother me. We don't have to worry about fixing the car, cleaning the house, paying our bills, or any of that crap while we're up there. We just float.

Mike: The big hyped-up gigs often aren't my favorites, and that's probably true for most of the

band. When we started touring in 1988, we played one landmark gig after another: the first time we played the Paradise in Boston, for example, or the first time we played for a thousand people, at the University of Massachusetts. When we played the Paradise, we'd never seen 650 people in a room before. Looking out at them through this little window before the gig was one of the most exciting moments of my life. But the show itself wasn't a peak musical experience at all; I remember it as raunchy noise. The following night, however, *was* a musical thrill because we'd been relieved of the pressure of playing a big rock club for the first time.

Trey: I keep learning the same lesson over and over again: We play best at shows in the middle of nowhere. We had a monumental show in some Tampa, Florida, shit hole, when this heavy-metal singer spontaneously jumped onstage and started screaming.

Mike: But so what if a show is hyped? I've heard that Janis Joplin would work herself into a frenzy before she went onstage. Ritual is a good thing to practice any night you play; it shows you care about what you're doing. During the four-night New Year's run, I always expect fans to prefer one of the middle shows to New Year's Eve itself. It's almost trendy not to prefer it.

Page: We'd already played three good shows in a row leading up to New Year's Eve and probably all assumed it would be an easy show because we'd been playing so well and now we had the built-in New Year's Eve energy. In the past, if we loved the set we'd just played, we'd go backstage and rave about it. If we didn't like it for whatever reason, Mike would tend to not say much, and Fish would blow off steam: "What were you thinking when you looked over at me? I hate it when you look at me that way!" Nowadays, if there's a problem, we basically try to talk each other down and return to ground zero. Over the years we've learned that these backstage conversations have more to do with our personalities than with the actual set.

Trey: Joe Walsh said in an interview once that arenas sound so different from anywhere else that you need to relearn how to play once you start working them. That's definitely true. Moving gradually from clubs to arenas was one of the best things that could have happened to us. Because everyone—both band and crew—had to relearn everything, especially how the air moves. Now I've really come to love hearing a slow song in a big room.

Page: We play more aggressively and confidently as a tour proceeds. During the fall 1996 tour, we left the East Coast but continued to play big arenas that were progressively less full as we traveled further outside our usual circuit. In response, we ended up playing with even more conviction, working harder, and taking more chances in order to harness the sort of energy level that comes automatically at a sold-out arena show. It was an interesting tour that went on a little longer than it might have. In the end we usually managed to rally and play our little hearts out.

Trey: During 1996 we were really trying to get to this kind of music we were hearing in our heads, a way of playing where everybody was an equal part of a grid. At the same time we were going

through transitional external changes, like adjusting to bigger rooms. Eventually, it all came to-gether when we stopped trying so hard.

ABOVE LEFT: Backstage, Fleet Center, December 31, 1996
ABOVE: Boston, 1990

Page: We've always tried to do something new at every show—to expand the repertoire, even if we only reworked a small part of a song or covered something as grandiose as "Bohemian Rhap-sody." Each time we played at Nectar's, or wherever, we would try to debut something new or de-velop a transition. It didn't happen every night, but that was the goal, and it happened a lot. In early '97, for example, we tried to take the rotation jam to new heights—learning how to write and play songs on instruments other than our own. We wouldn't know what to do with ourselves if we weren't working on new material. Sometimes we'll try to improve our slower, more ballady songs, such as "If I Could" or "Billy Breathes," in the practice room before a show. Usually we end up just beating a dead horse when we spend time trying to find out what's wrong with a song, because there *isn't* anything wrong with it. It's better for us to move ahead and develop new material. Older songs either work or they don't, which is why they come and go.

Trey: We have a tendency to bite off more than we can chew. After the ROTC Halloween dance we

played in '83, our second gig was a free show in the basement of the University of Vermont's Slade Hall. It said a lot about the direction the band would eventually take. We wanted to play original tunes right off the bat, and we also wanted our own light show. So one of Mike's earliest projects was a huge plywood box with switches on it that operated a rack of colored lights that hardly lit anything. We dragged in a huge curving geometric plane for a backdrop, then collected our various stereo speakers and hung them from the ceiling facing different directions. I was a DJ at WRUV at the time, and another DJ, our friend Anne Labruciano, mixed sound effects on six turntables while we played. It took us all day to load all this junk into Slade, and we played for about twenty people.

Mike: I spent Hanukkah and Christmas in the basement practicing "Bohemian Rhapsody" to a cassette while our guests socialized upstairs. I learn things like this with the help of a fairly mathematical process my former bass teacher Jim Stinnette helped me work out. First I figure out what position most of the notes are in, then I notate it using scale numbers rather than letters. If it starts on the fifth, rises to the flatted third, then returns to the tonic, I'll write *5, b3, b3, 1*—with parentheses to signify a cluster of notes. "Bohemian Rhapsody" was fairly simple compared to Trey's atonal fugues, which involve a lot of subtle position shifts. The technical process of learning the music and then singing along to a tape is good discipline for me. It aligns my mind.

Trey: During our fall tour I saw a *VH1 Flashback* video of Queen doing "Bohemian Rhapsody," and I remember saying "I think we should cover this tune," as a joke, to Fish. The next thing I know, I'm asking our production manager, Hadden Hippsley, if he can get us a gospel choir for New Year's Eve. A week later, he did. Fortunately, the choir was totally into it.

Mike: We'd played a few gigs and practice sessions during the fall of 1983, so we weren't exactly feeling things out for the first time when Trey returned to UVM in the fall of '84 after his semester off. He was eager to play again, so we talked about what we wanted to do. I stipulated that if I played with them, I'd want to play both covers and originals. Some of my favorite bands at the time played a lot of covers. Max Creek played a lot of Dead tunes, and Urban Blight, a funk band everybody except me ignored, covered the much-revered Average White Band. We always talk about getting away from our egos, but there's a certain egoism regarding who wrote whatever song you happen to be playing; so that's another part of the ego to do away with. The source of what you're playing shouldn't make any difference if you're attempting to be true to the moment.

The First Gig, ROTC dance, Harris-Millis Cafeteria, University of Vermont, Burlington, October 30, 1983

THE BAND'S COVERING "Bohemian Rhapsody" was hardly the first time Phish had copped another band's music. During the course of three Halloweens, they scrupulously reproduced both the spirit and letter of *The Beatles* (the so-called White Album), the Who's *Quadrophenia*, and Talking Heads' *Remain in Light*. Phish's renditions of these records served as musical *costumes* donned as a one-shot deal for the surprise and delight of their fans, who remained in the dark as to which album had been selected until the performance itself. A uniquely appropriate occasion for such appropriations, Halloween has its origins in the nearly two-thousand-year-old Celtic belief that between October 31 and November 2 a rift between the ancestors' world and that of the living appeared, creating a portal through which the dead visited the earth and the recently deceased could pass safely to the other side. At that time, writes Philip Carr-Gomm in *Elements of the Druid Tradition*, "the dead are honored and feasted, not as the dead, but as the living spirits of loved ones and of guardians who hold the root-wisdom of the tribe."

Each of these albums, by now-defunct bands, was released during a different decade (in 1968, 1973, and 1980, respectively); all three bands, like Phish, contained four core members; and, taken together, the three albums plot a tidy graph of Phish's rock roots. *The Beatles*, often characterized as the first record the four mop tops recorded as they were drifting apart, celebrated a band now obviously much larger than the sum of its parts. It rocks, folks, and avant-gardes as well as any pop artifact ever has, interspersing its overall optimism with prophetic moments of sheer dread ("You know that what you eat you are / But what is sweet now turns so sour"). In its diversity it sounds more like a *band* album than anything they'd done before.

Tom Marshall recalls Phish's Halloween 1994 performance at the Glens Falls Civic Center in New York as a turning point in his perception of Phish. "It was at the end of their long, *long* White Album set, and everyone was at the brink of 'This is almost too much music in one sitting (or standing)—even though it's great,' when suddenly they were doing 'Revolution 9,' and Fishman said the Yoko line, 'If . . . you become naked,' at which point he lifted up his dress to reveal *himself*, and danced around, and bubbles were everywhere, and the lights were pure sixties cartoon, and the band slowly walked off, waving, Jon still frolicking about, Page with his head in his hands. The audience didn't clap, laugh, or anything. The friend beside me said, 'Oh my God,' and then everyone started clapping and screaming for about ten solid minutes. It was a psychic mind jolt. It didn't really surprise or delight me, it just somehow sucked out some of my being and replaced it with a combination of elation and dread."

The album *Quadrophenia*, similarly, had merged the Who's four distinctive personalities into a single organism. As performed by Phish at Chicago's Rosemont Horizon on Halloween '95, Quadrophenia's music took precedence over its story line, emphasizing the album as sonic adventure. If any single work prefigures Phish's onstage exuberance, it's the Who's *Live at Leeds*, a roiling, clashing caterwaul of an album that would probably be fruitless to mimic. But *Quadrophenia* provided a brutal and relatively complex structure in which Phish could lose

BELOW: Show program for *Remain in Light*, the Omni, Atlanta, Georgia, Halloween 1996

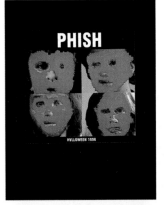

ABOVE: "If you become naked . . . ." Glens Falls Civic Center, Glens Falls, New York, Halloween, 1994

itself to a music that crashes onto its audience like wave after wave, with Pete Townshend's elemental themes and motifs repeated and transformed with raging hormonal torque.

Looking at the lyrics to *Remain in Light*, which Phish performed at the Omni in Atlanta on Halloween 1996, it's difficult to find a line that doesn't somehow jibe with the Phish aesthetic. It's an album of transition—a burning, breathing, shaking, swimming, drowning, dissolving, flowing experience. "Houses in Motion," indeed. With coproducer Brian Eno's assistance, David Byrne and Talking Heads rediscovered themselves as white guys who—surprise!—could reinvent themselves as delightfully loose white funkmeisters. Reflecting the disco and African influences that were in the air at the time they recorded *Remain in Light*, the Talking Heads' live performances of this music was revelatory for both band and audience. Fueled by the ecstasy of self-discovery, Byrne sang and played like a soul possessed, running the voodoo down and taking laps around the stage to celebrate his new sonic persona.

In performing music from *The Beatles*, Phish unmasked themselves as an eclectic band bigger than its parts; *Quadrophenia* symbolized their arena-rock ascent of '95 and '96, and *Remain in Light* foreshadowed the groove machine they'd become in 1997.

Fish: Instead of wearing real costumes onstage—which we'd done the past couple of years, although they rarely lasted more than a song or two—we decided to wear a musical costume in 1994.

Mike: One year at Goddard we dressed up as each other. Trey wore a very accurate Mike mask, and I dressed up as Trey's dog, Marley. Another year Fish shaved his entire body.

Fish: More than anything, covering an entire album is like taking a crash course in the band that made it. We always come away from the experience with much more than we thought we would.

Mike: The Halloween albums are like school. We usually start rehearsing the albums at home the last couple of weeks before we go on tour, then rent out practice space along the way.

One year we seriously considered doing an AC/DC album and getting the lead singer from a regional AC/DC cover band to sing for us because he looked and sounded exactly like Bon Scott. We contacted Roger Daltrey about singing *Quadrophenia,* since he'd already sung a Who song with the Spin Doctors, and we asked David Lee Roth to sing *Van Halen* with us, but they both turned us down.

Trey: The Beatles' White Album was part of my DNA when we did it in 1994. Having our fans vote again for the '95 Halloween album was a cool idea, but we suspect our pal Big Phil stuffed the ballot box for *Quadrophenia,* which got something like thirty-five votes out of the hundred or so cast. Fortunately, *Quadrophenia* was as much a part of Page's DNA as the White Album was of mine. The funny thing about *Quadrophenia* is that I didn't consider it that great an album even after our dress rehearsal. But it totally clicked for me as an arena masterpiece when we played it for a real audience.

Fish: The Beatles' White Album was chosen by the fans through mail-in votes. The first thing I realized when we were learning it was how much Pink Floyd drummer Nick Mason got from Ringo; he's Ringo with a little less swing. Ringo always sounds as though he's going for a clear musical idea, but then he flinches slightly at the last moment. So where Mason's riffs sound preconceived, Ringo sounds like he's playing right in the moment—and Charlie Watts always sounds just a little

late. I prefer higher, jazzier tones in my drums than Ringo used. He got a lot out of drums that were really loose: big, deep drums with thick heads he hit with fat sticks. What I learned from Ringo was how much could be achieved from so little. There are many points on the album where Ringo alters his pattern just a tiny bit but changes the sound significantly.

At first I thought "Revolution 9"—the White Album's collagelike next-to-last song—would be a good spot for the vacuum cleaner, since we wanted to create musical textures above which to recite the various lines. Since I had gotten naked onstage once before, during a "Battle of the Bands" at the Front in Burlington [4/21/89], everybody joked about my saying, "If you become naked. . . ," and then taking my dress off. But what I'd learned from my previous experience was that taking off your clothes really is the cheapest, laziest, and lamest way to get attention onstage. I felt it wouldn't have the same shock value if I did it again.

And yet, when I was standing there in my banana dress, something about the whole vibe in the room convinced me of the artistic relevance of whipping it off. It felt nice, even friendly. "If you become naked . . ." Well, what if? So I took off my dress, danced around, and felt completely free and liberated. It was probably the first time in rock history that somebody had gotten naked onstage and it wasn't for shock value.

Mike: The John Entwistle bass lines on *Quadrophenia* aren't necessarily fast or complicated, but they definitely jump around melodically. What I got from the album was the Who's immense *go-for-it!* attitude.

Fish: Ringo and Keith Moon lie at opposite ends of the drumming universe. Phish play pretty hard, but we play many different kinds of music, so there are hills and valleys during a show. The dynamics the Who worked, however, were all at the high end of the energy-output spectrum. I've never been more physically drained than after the *Quadrophenia* set.

I never played air drums to anything when I was a kid. But I'd put headphones on and play air guitar to the Who's *Live at Leeds* all the time. I'd get all juiced up on it, then go downstairs and play the drum parts with the album going through my head. Those guys must have been really tired after gigs. No wonder Moon was dead at thirty-one. His battery just ran out, like a wind-up toy that was overwound. If Trey looks like somebody playing air guitar with a real guitar, Keith Moon looked like somebody playing air drums with real drums.

Mike: The night we played *Remain in Light* was the first time I met my friend Steven Wright, the comedian. We had invited him to emcee the Clifford Ball, but he had a prior commitment. But Steven was still curious about us and came to the show in Atlanta. There was an interesting exchange in the dressing-room bathroom between Wright, who was in a stall, and Tom Marshall, who was in an adjacent stall. Steven was whistling something that to Tom sounded vaguely like Billy Joel's "Piano Man," so Tom asked, "Is that Billy Joel?" Wright replied, "I don't know . . ." To which Tom responded, "I wasn't referring to the song you were whistling. I meant, are *you* Billy Joel?" And Wright said, "That's what I meant." At which point Tom decided the funniest person in the world was behind the stall door; and he was right.

Goddard College Sculpture Building, Plainfield, Vermont, Halloween, 1987

Fish: If the Beatles were all about subtlety, and nobody rocks harder than the Who, *Remain in Light* was "Drumming and Singing at the Same Time 101" for me. There were so many layered vocal and instrumental parts on *Remain in Light* that there was simply no way for me to avoid singing. I *had* to. The album's drumming was consistent throughout entire songs, so after I learned the four percussive parts I usually do, I was able to add a fifth part—my voice—which essentially became a fifth limb. In general, I prefer to just play my drums. Now I'm eager to sing, and singing has become a good way to spice up a song that doesn't have a particularly interesting drum part. When we learn a new song with several different vocal parts, certain lines will jump out at me, and I'll try to grab them as a singer.

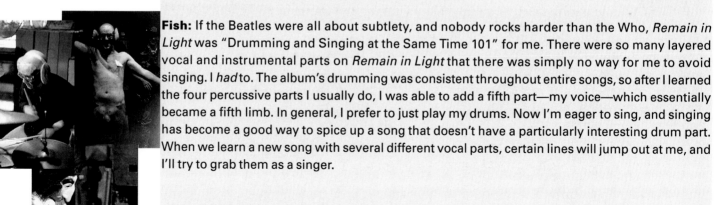

Mike: It made sense that we did *Remain in Light* right before a year in which we concentrated on sparser grooving jams, various synth textures, and cascading delayed cycles on top of it. *Remain in Light* probably stuck with us more in the short run than either of the other two Halloween albums.

Trey: The night before we did *Remain in Light,* the four of us had inched our way through each song, but we still hadn't made it through the entire album. I was really worried. We practiced for five or six hours that night, our first rehearsal with the horns, and only made it through the first

three tunes. I was exhausted, tense, and losing my voice at two in the morning before Halloween. We had a final rehearsal during sound check and finished it right before the doors opened. I tried to relax and get into gig mode, which for me is simply laughing and partying. But I was in organizational mode during the first set instead of just rolling my eyes back and drooling as usual. In the end, though, we completely nailed *Remain in Light.* I was out of my body during the set, overjoyed.

Rosemont Horizon, Halloween, 1995

Mike: Sometimes I find our faithfulness to cover versions a little weird. Part of me thinks, "Why not just go home and listen to the original record?" I guess it's fun to hear the song live with your friends at a Phish show. It doesn't necessarily matter to me whether I'm playing a cover or an original, so long as the tune opens up into a jam or takes on a subtle new attitude.

We've always liked fucking with people's minds. When we used to play fraternities, we'd perversely play worked-out music to people who expected Stones covers. I always liked staring directly into the eyes of someone freaked out by us playing these odd rhythms as though they were rock and roll. That still happens from time to time when we play to new audiences.

Trey: Mike has a funny way of getting what he wants. Early on he wanted us to cover a Max Creek bluegrass tune called "Back Porch." He knew we wouldn't do it, though, because not only weren't

we into playing covers at the time, but we probably wouldn't have done it even if we were. Nevertheless, he came to band practice in Fish's bedroom one day and suggested we write a bluegrass tune together. "A lot of bluegrass songs start with a riff like this," he began, "and maybe we could do it in the key of A." Over the course of a three-hour band practice Mike managed to convince us we were writing a bluegrass original with middle sections, complicated harmonized riffing, the works. Max Creek came to Hunt's about six months later, and most of the band went to their show. Mike was acting kind of weird, though, probably afraid they were going to play "Back Porch." And, lo and behold, they did. "That's funny," I thought. "Our bluegrass song starts just like this one." Then I thought, "Hey, they're playing our song!"

Page: Many of the songs we cover, like ZZ Top's "La Grange" or "Jesus Just Left Chicago" are largely excuses to jam. Josh White's "Timber Ho" is a traditional tune we really made our own with the beat we put on it, and our version of Duke Ellington's "Caravan" retains its jazz form.

Mike: I heard some of our fall '96 West Palm Beach show on the radio while I was driving one day. "A Day in the Life" came on, and I didn't know what song it was, who it was by, or what band was covering it—but I liked the way it sounded. My guess was that it was a Beatles song done by Aerosmith sometime in the seventies.

Fish: We respect tradition, but it's like a Borg thing. We take in all these different styles then apply them to original material so it comes out sounding different.

Mike: Trey and I have argued the continuity-versus-change issue extensively. I like the idea of extending the tradition, although I'm not into homages. I hate tribute bands that dress up like Led Zeppelin or the Doors. But picture some redneck bar in the South, with everyone wearing cowboy hats and drinking Jack Daniel's. When the country band sets up and plays old country songs, nobody's thinking, "Too bad they don't have their own material." Something alive and American is still going on there, a rich continuity. So I wanted to play some Little Feat songs, and Trey did too. For a while we played half covers and half originals. Over the years, though, I increasingly enjoyed going to band practice and learning original songs, even though I was the guy who wanted to play covers. I like being challenged intellectually. And now Trey likes playing cover songs.

Page: We perform Hendrix's "Fire," the Stones' "Loving Cup," Led Zeppelin's "Good Times Bad

ABOVE: Trey and Mike in New York City with their Languedoc guitars, June 29, 1995
OPPOSITE: Goddard College, Plainfield, Vermont, fall 1987

Times," and other classic rock hits much like the original versions, then do big Phish-style jams at the end. On the other hand, we radically changed the bluegrass standard "Uncle Pen." One of its lines goes, "First we played the tune called 'Soldier's Joy' / Then we played one called 'Boston Boy,'" and we actually stick those two songs in the middle. We also did a bluegrass version of the Boston tune "Foreplay"/"Long Time" where Mike learned the whole organ intro on banjo.

Mike : After Trey got kicked out of UVM in '83 and left town for a semester, Fish and I played with two guitarists from a band called the Dangerous Grapes. Dick lived in the Sigma Nu fraternity, which was bad news, the most dangerous fraternity on campus. But it was as peaceful as a New Age grocery store when we practiced there after school, even if you could still smell the puke from the night before. We'd watch the sun set majestically over Lake Champlain and play things like the Allmans' version of Willie Cobb's "You Don't Love Me," Stevie Ray Vaughn songs, a couple of Dead tunes, and some other blues-rock chestnuts. We weren't a very good band, but we seemed to groove magically nearly every afternoon we played.

When Trey returned to UVM, Fish and I discussed who we should play with. Fish said, "I'm playing with Trey." Fish is great at following strong energy, and Trey vibrates with original concepts and the energy to make them happen. The three of us played "In the Midnight Hour" for hours in the Wing Hall dorm lounge while people danced around. But while those first few practice sessions with Trey and Jeff Holdsworth were fun, they didn't click as much for me as they did for everyone else. I felt unsure about my role in the group. I couldn't keep up with all the guitar notes, and I had difficulty latching onto Fish's frenetic style.

Not clicking right off ended up being a good thing, however, because we ended up working harder to make it happen. Now, after more than fourteen years of practicing and sharing musical experiences together, we've become amazingly sympathetic to one another. And if the Grapes had stayed together, we wouldn't have gone anywhere no matter how well we clicked because there was no impetus to stretch our limits and write original songs. Clicking was all there ever really was.

Trey: Jeff Holdsworth had been in good bands during high school and was the most experienced and competent of us by far. He had an incredible bluesy voice and real stage presence that could knock you out right away. He was a grounding force, while Mike and I were more off-kilter. We didn't know any songs when we played our first gig at the UVM ROTC party [10/30/83] and had a week to come up with an entire repertoire. It ended up being all songs that Jeff knew, like "Long Cool Woman," "Proud Mary," and "I Heard It Through the Grapevine," which he also sang. But I wanted to do original stuff from the beginning, and he wasn't into it. Page joined the band about the same time I wrote "You Enjoy Myself," and we had a band practice in the little red house on King Street right across from the Harry Hood plant. I'd brought in sheet music with some of "You Enjoy Myself" on it, but Jeff was against it, while Page and the other two were totally into playing it. It was a defining moment and we knew something would have to give. I'd always felt something significant could come out of the band, but I think Jeff considered it more of a fun weekend thing. So when I added learning charts to the equation, he was like, "Forget it."

Fish: Mike was the odd man out early on. He always wanted to play more comfortably straight-ahead material, while the rest of us always tried to break new ground. We weren't necessarily breaking ground other people hadn't broken before us, but the idea was that if we kept breaking

ground for ourselves, eventually we might actually enter uncharted territory, which is all I want out of life. I like comfort, but I couldn't care less about being comfortable musically. Working with songwriters who continually write challenging music makes me a better drummer. Basically, I was in the right place at the right time. I'm a good drummer, but there are lots of good drummers out there.

Trey: Jeff was a fascinating guy, as I increasingly came to see. When we started playing together in 1983, he wore Ray-Ban sunglasses and cool belt buckles, and played a wicked guitar through a Marshall stack with all these effects—the whole rock-dude deal. Over the next couple of years, however, he ditched all his effects, substituted a tiny Fender Tweed for his Marshalls, and replaced his guitar strap with a rope before swearing off electric guitar altogether in order to devote himself to acoustic music. After Page joined in '85, an awkward period ensued during which we knew the four of us would go forward as a band, and he would eventually be out. But we had to keep doing gigs with five people. We definitely had a bad onstage vibe for a while.

After a hilarious Halloween gig during which some of us got so dosed we couldn't play, he left town, and I didn't see him for several months. The four of us moved to a house in Winooski, and one night there was a knock on the door. I open it to find a thin guy with a big button that said THE SON—JESUS around a picture of the sun. I didn't recognize Jeff at first. He had undergone a genuine transformation and looked completely different. He was thin and drawn, but he looked pretty content. We had just recorded *Junta,* so I played "David Bowie" for him. He made me turn it off two minutes into the jam, claiming that the Devil was making me play that kind of music. When I asked him where he'd been, he told me about driving across the country, ending up in Oregon, meeting a woman, and driving back across the country. He described some significant spiritual event and said, "That's when I saw the light." The moment he said that, a broken light above us that hadn't worked in months suddenly went on. He looked up, looked back down, and without missing a beat said, "Praise the Lord." We ran into him once a few years later in Philadelphia outside a gig at the 23 East Cabaret. We invited him in to play with us but he declined, and that was the last time we saw him.

Page: We try to showcase new material. Most of the people we play to live in whatever town we happen to be in and aren't following us across the country. It's a balancing act for us to please both the tour heads and the locals. Historically, however, we've always featured our new material more than the old stuff.

By the time we played "Bohemian Rhapsody," my voice was shot. It's an unbelievable arrangement, though, and I loved singing it in rehearsals. It didn't sound as bad as it might have, but I probably won't have another opportunity to sing it with a gospel choir in front of twenty thousand people.

Tom Marshall: Oh man, they killed it.

Trey: The funniest thing about Queen is that here's this flamboyantly gay man in a band called Queen, and now "We Will Rock You" is the football theme song of the world. That's even more ironic than rain on your wedding day.

Mike: The choir arrived between sets. I wandered into their rehearsal room and had a wonderful

When the revolution
occurs I must be
taken from an asylum
an allowed
to live!

Zane
Live.

Viva
La
Musik

experience before the rest of the band got there. The choir members, wearing bright red robes I hadn't seen, were singing gospel songs with their pianist. I picked up the bass and had my moment of glory playing gospel music with the choir and pianist, just me and them. I hoped the pianist would like the bass lines I came up with, so I kept looking over at him. I don't think he gave a damn, but I still had fun.

Trey: Queen's guitarist, Brian May, had a fat midrange sound instead of high, piercing, and distorted guitar tones. The only other guitarist who played with that kind of sound was Robert Fripp, and I've emulated both of them. May's sound definitely influenced the sustained notes I use in "Squirming Coil." I even tried using his Vox AC-30 amp for a while.

Suspicious minds:
Fish duels with
Elvis imperson-
ators, the Aladdin,
Las Vegas, Nevada
December 6, 1996

Fish: The "Rhapsody" improved as it went on, and Page did a damn fine job. He really stuck his neck out and sang it strong—both strong and right and strong and wrong. It took balls to sing in Freddie Mercury's gym like that. As far as I know, we're the only band—including Queen—to ever perform the tune live with a choir.

Trey: New Year's Eve is the perfect opportunity for conceptual hijinks. Frustrated that all the ideas we had for our '94 New Year's show sounded too bland, somebody made a joke about letting whoever had the worst seats during the show end up with the *best* seats in the house at midnight. How could we do this? Well, what if we flew across the room in a hot dog? You can never please everyone, unfortunately. One guy wrote us about how pissed off he was that the ticket price had gone up to twenty-five bucks, and he hated paying big money for dumb pranks when he really just wanted to hear music.

I'm so happy to be in a band that does shit like this. We've always alternated between playing relaxed shows and putting on fiascoes involving, for example, people pushing lawn mowers back and forth across the stage. For better or worse, we tend to follow through on spur-of-the-moment ideas. I heard "Cinnamon Girl" on the radio the afternoon we launched Phish Food at the Flynn Theater in Burlington. It's a completely unpretentious tune, not too hard to play, and maybe even too predictable a cover, but I loved it when I heard it and wanted to open the show with it. Our road manager, Brad Sands, ran out and found a copy, we rehearsed it backstage, and played it during the show an hour later.

Page: In our own way we're actually pretty theatrical for a rock band. We don't execute typical rock-band theatrics, banter, or prance around. Instead we freeze onstage or play silent jams. Even our basic presentation—how we arrive onstage, keep the show moving, and take a bow together—contributes to the theatrics of a show. But we also try to lose ourselves onstage and forget who we are, so even our spontaneity is theatrical in a funny way. Trey saw a lot of Broadway theater, and I sang in musicals

during high school. You could have seen me in *Once Upon a Mattress* and playing the title role in *Finian's Rainbow*.

Trey: We came up with idea after idea about how to take advantage of playing the capital of show-biz schmaltz in December 1996. For the Las Vegas show's encore we hired four Elvis imperson-ators to come out and engage in a vocal duel with Fish—who, by the way, kicked their asses. Mike had met a mother-daughter yodeling team who we also incorporated into the finale, along with Les Claypool and "Ler" [Larry Lalonde] from Primus. Some of our best ideas didn't come off, un-fortunately. I had asked our production manager, Hadden, to get a few dozen showgirls and a white Siberian tiger for the "Harpua" encore. When we sang the last chord of the song—"*a dog!*"—I wanted to have the showgirls do a kick line as the white tiger walked onstage. Right be-fore the encore, though, I learned that the theater management wouldn't allow the tiger onstage. I'd also imagined the showgirls wearing big, feathery Vegas costumes. But when I went back-stage, it looked as though Hadden had just called an escort service. Dozens of what appeared to be scantily clad hookers were wandering around and I thought, "Naah."

Mike: In the early nineties, we sometimes stood in front of baffled college crowds repeating the same five-note phrase for ten minutes. Each cluster of notes would be interrupted by the word "wait," as though we had screwed up and wanted to start fresh. After four minutes, an incredibly long time at a concert, people looked up blank-faced; after six minutes people started yelling; after eight minutes they started screaming "Fuck you!" along with the word "wait"; and by ten minutes they had returned to blank stares.

THIS PAGE AND OPPOSITE:
Myndy K. and Spiral
Force, Rock-L as the
Merengue Butterfly
Princess, Shelly Bomb
and the Vibrating
Circus, Willie Ninja
and Extravaganza,
and Fabian and
Wynona join the band
at Madison Square
Garden, October 22,
1996

Trey: We spend a lot of time on the bus concocting pranks we play both onstage and off. My very favorite originated when Mike picked up a hitchhiker who turned out to be Courtney Gains, the actor who played the demonic, red-headed Malachai in the movie *Children of the Corn.* Mike and Courtney became friends, and we came up with the idea of using Courtney, who still looks just like he did in the movie, to play a joke on somebody. So when we played Las Vegas for the first time in December 1996, I stayed in an enormous two-floor Caesars Palace suite decorated with leopard-skin rugs and ceiling mirrors, and hosted a huge party the night before the gig. Our plan was to take my friend Chris Cottrell downstairs to gamble at one in the morning. We'd both been partying all night, eating mushrooms, the whole bit. While we were downstairs, Mike cleared everybody out of the room and cued up *Children of the Corn* on the large-screen TV. When I returned to the suite with Chris, at around three, the room was totally dark and empty except for Mike, who was watching the movie. We sat beside him on the couch just in time to enjoy Malachai gorily hacking some people to death. After the scene, Mike said good night and hid in another room, so it was just me and Chris.

I said I was going to the bathroom but instead went into the bedroom and exchanged my bright blue jacket and other funky Vegas clothes with Courtney, who we'd flown in from Los Angeles for the occasion. Malachai, now dressed as me, came out of the bedroom and sat beside Chris on the couch. After a minute or so, Chris turned away from the TV, noticed Courtney sitting beside him, got real quiet, then calmly said, "Malachai!" Instead of screaming or running out of the room, which we'd expected, he stood up and slowly backed away from Courtney. We'd also hired a pair of opera singers to hide in the balcony and let loose with a blood-curdling chord to add to the insanity when Chris lost it. Unfortunately, he didn't react enough for them to take their cue. He just calmly walked out of the room, down the hall, and right into me. The first thing to come out of my mouth was, "Did you know this was going to happen?" I thought I might have accidentally mentioned the prank to him during the many months we'd been planning it, but I hadn't. So it sounded to Chris as though I meant, "Did you know Malachai was going to come out of the TV screen and sit beside you on the couch?"

Mike: I loved the flamboyant dancers our friend Myndy K. brought on-stage at Madison Square Garden [10/22/96]. Myndy also taught us the dance steps we do in "Guelah Papyrus" and "Punch You in the Eye." Then there was the time my friend Andrea Baker, a bald black singer in a white robe from the San Francisco Opera Company, sang Puccini's "O Mio Babbino Caro" in San Francisco [5/27/94]. At the end of the aria she handed a box of macaroni and cheese to a two-year-old in the front row. Then we passed out two thousand more boxes to the rest of the audience to create a huge percussion ensemble.

Trey: We used to practice in this tiny, dingy, one-room efficiency apartment Page had in a place called the Castle. He had some old graying barbershop-quartet music we decided to learn as a goof. It turned out to be a terrific idea once we started playing theaters and could sing these songs unmiked. It became an intimate way to connect with the audience, so we kept doing it in bigger and bigger venues, the largest of which was for six thousand people on New Year's Eve '92 in

Boston, and it worked. And since people always complain that we don't cover enough music from the nineties, we did—only it was from the *1890s*! The theory behind barbershop quartets is that anybody can sing, something we demonstrate every time we play.

Mike: We started singing barbershop quartets because, one, we are, after all, a quartet, and two, we like to break up the show. We started with some old arrangements Page owned. Then it turned out his landlord was a vocal coach in the Society for the Preservation and Encouragement of Barber Shop Quartet Singing in America. The goal in barbershop singing is to make four singers sound like more through vocal resonance. When the harmonies are really working, you can hear operatic vocal overtones. Page's landlord gave us two posters of mouth shapes associated with vowel sounds—your mouth should be square-shaped when you sing the vowel A, for example—and taught us how to synchronize our breathing. Our biggest problem, he said, aside from not blending well, was that we breathed too often. He ridiculed our old arrangements and provided us with some newer, hipper ones.

Fish and I went down to one of the society's monthly meetings at the Knights of Columbus Hall. There were about sixty people there, and although we could barely read music, they immediately stuck us in two different groups standing on bleachers, handed us music, and helped us muddle through five or ten songs in about an hour—this after us having learned exactly one song with the band during the past two months. Then they announced they had guests in the house—"Jon and Mike from Phish"—and brought us down in front of everyone for their "standard welcome." We were terrified they would make us sing for the group; instead, they sang, "We welcome you to our place." As they sang, they descended from the bleachers single file, shook our hands, and then returned to the bleachers, singing all the time. At one point everyone took a break to share "tags" with one another. Tags are four-bar intros or endings to songs. We begin "Sweet Adeline" with a tag that goes, "You're the flower of my heart, sweet Adeline," and then sing the rest of the song.

The most memorable part of the experience, for me anyway, was being in a room that *really* smelled like aftershave lotion.

Trey: The '96 New Year's Eve show was a turning point for us. It was fun—it's *always* fun—but it was an intensely planned and methodical kind of fun. New Year's '97, in contrast, was one big glorious blur for me. It's strange. There are some shows that crystallize into great experiences for both us and the audience, and I usually remember about a minute of them.

That New Year's Eve show was important to us in at least one way: It inspired us to get together and change into the more purely musical ensemble we started becoming in Europe the following February. We'd been imagining a different kind of music even before this show, and were already changing in our heads. I remember West Coast shows before the New Year's show that suggested how our ideas about what the band could be had already preceded our ability to do it. So we were still relying on our old bag of tricks to get us through some of these gigs.

Voters for Choice
benefit concert, Lowell
Memorial Auditorium,
Lowell, Massachusetts,
May 16, 1995

I MIGHT BE ON A SIDE STREET: EUROPE

IN FEBRUARY 1997 Phish followed their first all-arena tour with a fourteen-show run through Europe, the group's first headlining tour on the continent. The band and a pared-down crew relived their first years together by working exclusively in clubs and small theaters, playing to a funny melange of locals and itchy-sweatered Americans abroad in assorted venues, many of which converted into discos as soon as the musicians left the stage. The tour offered Phish the long-awaited opportunity to perform "You Enjoy Myself" in Florence (2/21/97), the city that inspired the song's most inscrutable lyric. Stuttgart (2/25/97) was a hard-core fan satisfier that included such scarcities as a "Camel Walk" opener, "Tube," and "Magilla." The show in Hamburg's Markthalle (3/1/97), on the other hand, was momentous for the band, marking a musical turning point that was edited down and released in October 1997 as the album *Slip Stitch and Pass.*

Phish introduced the band-written tunes "Walfredo," "Rock-a-William," and "Carini Had a Lumpy Head." The band members switched instruments to perform the first two of these, and all three songs contained autobiographical lyrics—concerning a Santana percussionist and a friend in Colorado among other subjects—in the longstanding rock tradition of taking verbal snapshots of life on the road.

Phish makes touring itself another element in an alchemical reaction achieved by combining moment, material, and audience. In their embryonic form, Phish often performed on the UVM and Goddard College campuses in 1985 and 1986, as well as in such Burlington bars as Hunt's, Nectar's, and the Front. The band's breakout from highly popular local band to regional favorites came in 1989 when, unable to get a gig at Boston's Paradise (despite having played the Boston bar Molly's twice in the preceding three months), the band rented the venue themselves for a January 26 show. Longtime fan Tom Baggott recalls how "me and a guy named Brother Craig sold a busload of seats to our Burlington friends (we needed two buses the next time they played there). It was a Greyhound luxury liner, complete with stereo. As we

Nectar's,
Burlington, fall
1988

boarded, I handed the driver a hundred-dollar tip. He said, 'I don't see anything, I don't hear anything, I don't smell anything. Have a nice trip.' Well, it so happened that about half the people on the bus actually were tripping."

As early as 1989, recalls Paul Languedoc, "John Paluska was booking gigs in places other bands rarely played," such as cafeterias, dorms, frat houses, and even unlikelier college venues. "After we played the Paradise in Boston several times, John—very smart move—started looking around for alternative venues. He realized our audience was more interested in hearing the band than buying drinks, so he wisely decided to go for theaters." Paluska took a gamble that paid off. Playing theaters, the band was able to not only keep the gate but maintain tighter artistic control of shows that were growing progressively more ambitious—both musically and theatrically. The band played the Somerville Theatre on the outskirts of Boston in September 1990, sold out San Francisco's Great American Music Hall in October 1991 (without benefit of a nationally distributed album), and were playing theaters almost exclusively the following year. By 1994 Phish had outgrown these venues entirely and was forced to graduate to arenas. "But you have to remember," says Anastasio, "we slept on floors for six years."

In their transition from bars to theaters, Phish more resembled the honking and shouting rhythm-and-blues bands of the forties and fifties than they did their postpunk contemporaries. And for a few years during the mid-eighties, Burlington flourished as no less active a rock breeding ground than R.E.M.'s Athens in the late seventies or Chicago's so-called postrock scene today—only with a lot less hype. Phish—along with friends like Ninja

Custodian and the Joneses, as well as Pinhead, the Decentz, the Hollywood Indians, and the X-Rays—thrived in a quirky, eclectic, and inbred scene that also included its metal heads (Run 21, Screaming Broccoli) and a small yet influential jazz contingent. Anastasio and Fishman lived a block away from the Winooski, Vermont, club Sneakers, where they spent Tuesday nights listening to a house jazz band featuring James Harvey, Dave Grippo, and Russ Remington, and other musicians who have occasionally backed Phish as the Giant Country Horns.

Other locally popular East Coast bar bands—such as Blues Traveler, Widespread Panic, and the Aquarium Rescue Unit—were all breaking out of their respective scenes around the same time. In 1992 Blues Traveler leader John Popper created HORDE (Horizons of Rock Developing Everywhere) as a way for rock bands that shared the improv/groove aesthetic to market themselves nationally as a package, and Phish joined on for several shows.

Playing theaters, Phish gained a not entirely unfounded reputation as something of a novelty band that sang barbershop-quartet chestnuts as well as an a cappella version of "Free Bird" (with vocalized guitar solos). They were a four-person psychedelic extension of the vaudeville tradition in which audiences expected and received several different varieties of

The Giant Country Horns: (LEFT TO RIGHT) Russell Remington, Carl Gerhardt, and Dave Grippo, Townsend Family Park, Townsend, Vermont, July 14, 1991

entertainment for the price of a single ticket. Their weekly jazz gigs at the Drenched Cat in Burlington as the Johnny B. Fishman Jazz Ensemble during 1988 provided them with enough practice to make it through jazz standards like "Take the A Train" and "Caravan." They next turned their attention to bluegrass. Former Aquarium Rescue Unit member Reverend Jeff Mosier joined Phish on their tour bus in fall 1994. His instruction inspired the band to delve more frequently into their repertoire of American roots music, which included bluegrass and traditional tunes like "Nellie Cane" and the Dillards' "Old Home Place," and to more frequently punctuate their shows with acoustic segments.

Seeing Phish in a Rome theater or a Florence disco during the February 1997 European tour, I thought while savoring these shows, was the perfect way to experience the band as they might have appeared a decade earlier. Only better. In Europe Phish toured exclusively in clubs and small theaters for the first time in more than five years. When we spoke afterward, the band members reflected on some of their earlier forays outside the Burlington area.

Mike: My fiancé Cilla Foster was responsible for our first tour. In 1988 she was waitressing in Telluride, Colorado, for a guy named Warren Stickney. I didn't know her very well at the time, but one day she called and said Stickney wanted us to come play in his bar. We'd never played further away from home than New Hampshire at the time, but Stickney promised to book a monthlong tour across the country. It took another six months to get him on the phone again, but I finally spoke with him about a week before we were supposed to hit the road. He said something like, "I don't know if I can get you any other gigs, but you can play my place and I'll pay you a thousand bucks." I couldn't get him on the phone after that, so the six of us—including Paul Languedoc and Tim Rogers, who was doing lights—decided to go for it anyway. We finished playing a Nectar's gig at 2 A.M., took a vote, and decided to head west then and there. Our friends Ninja Custodian subbed for us the next night at Nectar's, and we took off across the country with turkey ham, cheese, and apple butter. It was the middle of summer, and we were traveling in a windowless truck with only a foam mattress on the floor. We didn't even stop at a rest area for forty hours, so the truck got pretty disgusting.

When we got to the edge of Colorado, maybe eight hours away from Telluride, we met some people who'd heard of Stickney, and learned about his reputation as a guy who didn't pay either his workers or his taxes. When we got to Telluride, there were posters with pictures of him all over town that said BABY HUEY GO HOME. Everyone wanted him to leave, but he wasn't even around and we didn't know if we had a gig or not. So we made our own posters advertising us as NEW ENGLAND'S MOST NAIVE ROCK & ROLL BAND. WE DROVE 2,000 MILES BECAUSE WARREN STICKNEY PROMISED US A THOUSAND BUCKS. Stickney seemed kind of bummed about them when we finally met him, but he admitted that, given his reputation, we had a point. He ended up actually paying us a thousand bucks—except for a $155 check that bounced—but we had to play ten nights to earn it. We stayed on the floor in a house called the Purple Palace. Cilla had lived there, but she'd moved away before we arrived in town.

Fish: We played to the same dozen people at the Roma for ten nights. The whole town was boycotting the place because of Stickney's reputation. We didn't realize the impact the boycott was having until someone said, "A lot of people want to see you, but they won't go to the Roma. We're not boycotting the Fly Me to the Moon Saloon, though. Why don't you play there?" So on our day off from the Roma, we carried our equipment across the street and played at Fly Me to the Moon, which was owned by somebody else. It was a weeknight but the place was completely packed, and they ran out of alcohol during the evening. The next day we moved our gear back across the street to the Roma and played the rest of our gigs there to more or less empty houses.

Mike: Stickney managed to get us a gig in Aspen on our way home. We stayed with a friend of a former roommate of Fish's, but we made the mistake of leaving all our money in a folder in the kitchen, and someone stole it. Other than that, our first tour was a raging success.

Trey: We did our first all-arena tour in fall '96. It was successful in some ways, and unsuccessful in others, but it helped make us comfortable in our own skin with playing large rooms. We had to ask ourselves, "How can we make this transition and still be the same band we always were? How can we maintain the same musical ideals as when we were playing clubs?" It so happened that our next two tours would consist mainly of clubs and theaters in Europe, which not only reminded us where we came from, but proved to me that even if I only did that for the rest of my life, I'd be thrilled. These tours got us back in touch with the looseness that's always been part of Phish, and I think we brought these renewed feelings of spontaneity and intimacy back into the bigger rooms we played that summer.

Page: We didn't just say, "Let's play some clubs!" We've always enjoyed developing new audiences, and short Europe tours seemed like a natural step to take in that direction.

Mike: Awhile back, after a band meeting in town, I went over to Club Toast to see this great bluegrass guitar player named Doug Perkins and his band, Smokin' Grass. I went into the bathroom, which was covered with graffiti, and thought, "The band sounds pretty good, there are some hippie-ish people hanging out, and the bathroom smells bad. Wow, I'm totally in my element here." But it was kind of an old element, like when I was a college student going to bars. But if it takes me up to a certain level, why not still do it, even if I feel old? Why let social awkwardness get in the way of a good time?

Trey: We stopped trying so hard in '97, and it was the best thing we could have done. Everybody else in the band seemed to step out a little bit more. 'Ninety-seven turned out to be a real celebratory year. 'Ninety-six felt more like a work year in a funny way. We were trying really hard to accomplish something and then this year we stopped trying and just went onstage and played.

BELOW: Spear Street party, South Burlington, Vermont, May 21, 1988
BOTTOM: Assface, Boston, Massachusetts, 1991

LIKE OTHER GROUPS influenced by the surprisingly durable blues-rock improvisations of the Grateful Dead and the Allman Brothers, Phish modeled their music on conversational jams that told stories and spiraled upward to profound heights of Saturday-night release. But Phish took this model one step, then several steps, further, looking to Africa, Latin America, and the black and white pop sounds found in their own backyard for inspiration. More important, they spent long rehearsal-room hours searching for something personal yet ego-transcending, a way of performing that erased habit and cliché.

A line from "The Wedge"—"We're bobbing on the surface, and a shadow glides below"—nicely reflects a rich Phish jam. It's a world of light and dark, of floating and gliding, of swimming and drowning, with all the tints and hues in between. It's the blissed-out implied violence of "Free": "I'm floating in the blimp a lot, I feel the feeling I forgot . . . / In a minute I'll be free, and you'll be splashing in the sea." At their best, Phish's jams wander effortlessly between bliss and despair, a four-way dreamworld of subsurface visions and stream-of-consciousness sound that trickles, flows, and then pours into oceanic release.

Photo collage by former road manager Andrew Fischbeck, September 13, 1990, to July 28, 1991

Trey: You can't hear what's going on without leaving space in the music. I can't communicate without space. It's more powerful than notes. Nervous energy causes overplaying, which comes off as nothing but a series of notes no one can follow. You need space to join, to meld. I like to communicate, so I'm always looking at somebody when I'm onstage. It doesn't matter whether it's another band member or someone dancing in the audience, because if I'm communicating with anybody, if we're really having a conversation rather than a monologue, everyone hears and feels it.

Mike: I dreamed that Trey and I were playing Bad Company's "Can't Get Enough" on wireless guitars. We were on the floor, talking to people in front of the stage while we played. "Hello. How's it going? What's up?" I really liked that. It's as though we were all in it together, rather than separate from the audience.

Page: The goal is to achieve more through less. When I hear tapes, I often wish I'd played half the notes I did. Sometimes playing a lot of piano notes just creates a wash of noise in the mix. But if I play a single perfectly placed note, you'll hear it. Less can indeed be more, and there's plenty of noise up on that stage even when just one of us is playing.

Mike: Another common thing we criticize one another for is not being solid, and solid includes simple. This poses an interesting paradox for a bassist. If I'm sensitively playing only what I'm hearing, but I'm not hearing anything yet and therefore not playing much, then the group's solidity suffers through me not entering the music decisively with something substantial enough for the others to work with. Our best jams occur when we start with something so solid, so basic, that it can go anywhere. If we don't have a firm foundation, the jams just wander.

Sometimes I'll play a few notes for a long time and things will take off. Other times I worry the guys are thinking, "He's not listening. He's just playing the same notes over and over." I remember doing this once while we were playing "Harry Hood" somewhere down South. I found these two notes I liked near the beginning of the jam. They weren't in the root of the key we were in, but I really liked the way they sounded. But I began to sense frustration from other band members, who afterward told me they hated what I'd been playing. They said, "We can't believe you played those two notes the whole time. It was horrible."

Fish: We're pretty good about offering feedback. We've always striven for honesty concerning our respective weaknesses. Whenever we identify a weakness, we make an effort to address it and transform it into a strength. For example, it became obvious somewhere along the line that the bottom was falling out of our jams a lot. We could really stretch things out, but we weren't necessarily great about establishing a good place to stretch out from. The music lacked the contrast of being out there in the context of a solid origin.

Trey: Page flounders less than anyone. He's Mr. Even Keel. Mike is a little moodier by nature; he'll have great highs and great lows. Everyone in our band becomes naked to one another during the jams. You can clearly hear what each of us is thinking. It's like having the most intimate conversation imaginable, and it just becomes more so the longer we're together.

Fish: I always picture a brain floating in a container of water, and the music is all the liquid sur-

OPPOSITE : Boston, 1990
ABOVE: Boston. 1991

rounding it. Your brain has to float in the middle of the pool if you want to really hear everything. If you focus on one aspect of the music, it's as though the liquid dries up or drifts toward one specific zone. After eight years of listening to Trey, and then focusing on Page for a while, it finally occurred to me, "Gee I wonder what the bass player is doing?" It was really as dumb as that. I always took Mike for granted.

Trey: For the most part, drums are easier to play than guitar, mainly because you don't have to think about notes. And it's all right there in your body; if you're feeling good, you're banging good. It's like punching the light bag or hitting a tennis ball. Fish plays shit that nobody plays. He's totally loose; his playing never sounds like a riff, and the three of us just try to keep up with him. When we used to play at Nectar's, he and I would play rhythm tag to the point of annoying the other guys, and we've had a lot of wonderful experiences playing drum duels in Goddard's music building. I've considered getting a Junior Pro set like Adrian Belew had during his second King Crimson tour. There'd be Fish, a little guy with a big drum set, and me, a bigger guy with a little set.

Fish: For a long time every jam had to end with a big bang, which is inevitable whenever we take our time and smell the roses along the way. Sometimes nothing will happen for a while, and we'll become insecure and freak out, bail out, or try to force excitement. But the big bang should be more the consequence of a process rather than the goal.

Mike: Trey's rhythm guitar and Fish's high-hat drove the band for years. But Trey gets frustrated when he feels he's strumming just to hold the beat. He's got a great sense of rhythm, but I've learned a lot over the years. I may be our most improved player.

Trey: The first thing I try to do onstage is stop thinking, so I need to internalize all the harmonic theory I know. The trick is to practice something until it becomes second nature, then forget it. Joe Pass—absolutely the greatest chordal genius to play the guitar—recommended never practicing anything hard, because you'll want to play it onstage just to justify the time you spent learning it. "Practice music," he said, which had a profound effect on me. You'd think Joe Pass would know thousands of complicated chords. But from his point of view there are only three chords: major, minor, and dominant—the five chord. Everything else is just sound colors we pick up along the way. Pass said he learned guitar by sitting in front of the radio with his father. A song would come on, and his dad would say, "Play that." That's really the best way to learn to play any instrument.

I knew what I was doing with tension and release on an instinctual level long before I learned the theory behind it. Figuring out why it works in theory simply enabled me to take it further in practice.

Mike: I often think of the bass in terms of high and low. I try to go beyond notes and scales, and concentrate instead on up and down or before and after. The high notes don't have a lot of vibration while the low notes do. Rather than going up-down, up-down, a jazz bassist playing a good walking bass line will go up-up-up-up, down-down-down-down. I'll take a song like "Cars Trucks Buses," which started out with an organ bass line, then see how I can change it and how it will be affected by those changes.

Phil Lesh might be my favorite bass player. He's melodic and supportive at once. I never sat down and learned his bass lines because I didn't want to be that specifically influenced by how he played. I was onstage one of the last times I saw him play. The Dead's monitor mixer gave me headphones and I could push a button to hear each band member's headphone mix or isolate individual instruments. I only listened to the bass, and it really blew me away. Lesh's playing was actually a lot more repetitive than he claimed, and it sounded really Zenlike in isolation. A standard way to construct a bass line is to define the root every measure or two and then play higher notes in between. I do this—maybe too often. But one thing I picked up from Lesh is that your line has a lot more impact when you start with a high note, embellish it with low notes, and then return to the high note.

Trey: We have a three-hour window of music to fill, so variety is important. We all have a tendency to play all the time, so we've been working on laying out and backing off. It's only begun to sink in recently. Page plays a greater array of keyboard sounds now, especially his Fender Rhodes and synthesizers, and orchestration makes things more interesting if you're going to jam all night long. It's sometimes hard for me to drop out. The other three guys got used to me assuming a leadership role, so when I lay back, the jam tends to come down with me. I'm trying to get to the point where I can back off and see myself as poking in and out of the mud. Old habits die hard, but one of my favorite things about the band is that we really try to shake our routines.

We have a new dropping-out exercise: Two of us jam at a time while the other two listen. So Fish and Mike will groove for a while, then Mike and I, then Page and I, and so on. We've found that different combinations are more troublesome than others. Page said that playing with Mike was the hardest combination for him. We're still uncovering interesting little quirks about ourselves.

Page and Mike used to give Fish and me shit in the beginning while the two of us were having this little onstage love affair. Then I discovered Mike, and suddenly we harmonized bass and guitar all night long, night after night, for about a year and a half. Finally I discovered Page, and now I mainly listen to him when we jam. I already know the other two.

Mike: I played my Languedoc bass almost exclusively until the Hamburg show that ended up on *Slip Stitch and Pass.* I noticed that if I played up high, it sounded great and cut through everything else. But the low notes lacked definition; there was no high end in the Languedoc's low notes. Then, since we were in a club rather than an arena, I decided to switch basses and picked up my Modulus. All of a sudden even the low notes had definition—not all the low notes on the B string, but most of the low notes I play a lot. It sounded great, with an attack I hadn't been able to get before. When I heard the tape of the show's radio mix, it sounded just as I'd experienced it onstage.

Fish: Our band definitely evolved backward for me. Traditionally, rhythm sections are conscious of one another right from the start. They make a bed the other instruments rely on. But I related more strongly to the guitar from the start. Trey and I would go off on these duo excursions because I could always hear where his thoughts were going, especially rhythmically. When Page came along, I made a conscious effort to listen to him because he was the new guy. In a certain sense, Mike was always our rhythm anchor because he preferred playing less busily and could lay a foundation. Mike was the last guy I focused on, and now it's developed for me to the point where I hear all four of us as one really weird multilayered instrument.

Mike: Our best stuff used to come out of sound checks when we didn't feel obliged to play cool drumbeats, and it ended up being completely fresh and funky, and we'd just sink ourselves into the groove. Playing gigs was about keeping a high energy level while providing variety. Both of these things are important, and I'm glad we did them. But during a sound check Fish might play some old rock drumbeat that's been played sixty billion times already and not care whether he's being original or not, while I'll just dig into the bass line, and it ends up being the most original-

Shepherds Bush Empire, London, England, July 11, 1996

Trey's dog Marley
and the band,
Boston. 1991

sounding stuff we do, even though it starts from the simplest and least innovative beginnings.

Trey: I heard a jazz profile of George Shearing on National Public Radio recently. Shearing, the master of elegantly spacious arrangements, was asked what he thought of singer Mel Torme, with whom he'd worked. Shearing said, "The best. We breathed together." Then they interviewed Torme about Shearing, and he said the same thing. He said, "I've never played with anyone so sensitive in my life. He knows every move I'm going to make. We breathed together." We're capable of that, too.

Mike: I try to play with as little ego as possible by taking away as many notes as I can—maybe those are the ego notes. When I'm playing an eight-note pattern, it's going to sound even better if I can remove three of those notes and dig even deeper into the five I'm still playing. It's more than a method, it's an awareness. I once talked to Jim Stinnette about grooving. He said that while grooving couldn't be taught, there were certain things I could do to prepare myself for it, like keep my fingers limber, learn different styles of music, get enough sleep, or even deprive myself of sleep. It's almost as though a way of life, or a way of meditating, makes grooves more likely to occur.

Trey: "Tweezer" began as a sound-check jam. Mike and I kind of looked at each other as we were playing one day and started laughing.

BY FALL 1994, "Tweezer" had become an increasingly long and open-ended way for the band to explore the outer reaches of improv rock while cultivating vivid simplicity. In 1995, however, Anastasio assembled Surrender to the Air as a side project to experiment with improvisation at its freest and most spontaneous, music not necessarily bounded by rhythm, harmony, or groove. Thus Anastasio's dream team—consisting of Anastasio, saxophonist Marshall Allen, flutist Kofi Burbridge, bassist Oteil Burbridge, percussionist Damon R. Choice, Jon Fishman, drummer Bob Gullotti, trombonist James Harvey, keyboardist John Medeski, trumpeter Michael Ray, and guitarist Marc Ribot—spent two days in the studio in April 1995 and improvised for hours on end with neither preconceptions nor expectations. Following the eponymous record's release in March 1996, the band performed at New York City's Academy on April 1 and 2.

Beginning with occasional Phish accompanist Gullotti's delicate drum solo, *Surrender to the Air* passes through moods and moments often reminiscent of Sun Ra's Arkestra (with whom Allen, Ray, and Choice have been associated). More afrological than eurological, it winds through corridors of rhythm and mystery, dallying occasionally when three or four members become engaged in subtle conversations, before exploding into celebratory wailings from the urban jungle and then coming to rest. The biggest surprise on *Surrender to the Air* was the way in which Anastasio lurked just beneath the surface, assiduously abdicating authority and abandoning himself to music that sounded quite unlike anything else.

Fish backstage at La Laiterie, Strasbourg, France, June 24, 1997

Trey: In 1994 we went through a long period of extended improvisations that culminated in the thirty-five-minute "Tweezer" that landed on *A Live One*. After that "Tweezer" I decided to get the endless-jam idea out of my system, so I did *Surrender to the Air*. That influenced Phish in lots of strange and subtle ways, and it certainly influenced the crap out of me.

Surrender to the Air was the opposite of everything I'd been doing up until then, an entirely different musical ocean. At Goddard I studied orchestration and form with Ernie Stires, who must have told me a million times that freely improvised music was utter shit. But it was an authentic learning experience for me to just stand beside such highly respected improvisers as Marshall Allen and Marc Ribot. On the album, my plan was to improvise first, then to create form later by editing. I asked the band to play some short transitional bits that I used later as musical glue to join different sections of the jams. All I did backstage before the shows was try to keep the musicians from planning anything—and we did it. The shows were everything you would expect, complete with some incredible ups and dreadful downs. It was like being naked. Afterward I remember walking back to my hotel and thinking, "Well, I don't need to do *that* again."

Page: We don't play "Tweezer" as much as we did a few years ago, when we were consciously trying to stretch our jams out. "Tweezer" lent itself to that very well. We didn't intend to make the Bangor "Tweezer" [11/2/94] half an hour long. On the other hand, there have been "David Bowie"s where we said, "Let's see how far we can stretch it out." It takes a conscious effort sometimes, since we were inclined to play ten- or fifteen-minute "Bowie"s and not take that *extra* ten or fifteen minutes. Once in Dallas [5/7/94] we decided to play "Tweezer" for the whole set, which was probably the beginning of our whole extended-song thing. But a lot of those jams weren't very good in the end. When we were choosing material for *A Live One,* I'd hear these "Bowie"s, "Tweezer"s, and "Antelope"s and think, "That's a good moment there, but man, the next five minutes kind of drags."

Mike: I came up with the bass line for "Tweezer," Trey came up with the guitar part instantly, and we had a groove. We finished it at a Wetlands sound check and came up with the words spontaneously. I didn't particularly enjoy playing the Bangor "Tweezer" jam. But I loved hearing it on tape.

Trey: *Surrender to the Air* taught me how not to lead as much. I was surprised to hear complaints that I didn't play enough guitar on the album, because I'm playing almost the entire time. My role in that particular group of musicians was to be supportive, and I'm trying to do it more in Phish. I like laying back in the mush, with my guitar peeking out of the mud. When I hear tapes of us, the first thing I think is that I wish the guitar was mixed lower.

Fish: Our music invents a geography. It draws a big map. It starts out on land, where we build the boat, which is the written and arranged part of the music, the launching pad. Once we get into the water, we're like Columbus. We don't know the next time we're going to hit land, how wide the body of water is, or even whether we're crossing a lake or an ocean. It's more like dumping the vessel into the water than launching it gracefully. Sometimes we have to bail for a while before we actually get going.

Trey: The first thing Phish did after *Surrender to the Air* was *Billy Breathes,* which was anything

TOP: The Great Went, Limestone, Maine, August 16, 1997

ABOVE: Madison Square Garden, New York, New York, December 31, 1997

Outside the
Waartesaal,
Cologne, Germany,
February 16, 1997

but freely improvised. I wanted to remove material rather than add layers of detail. I recalled Brian Eno saying the twenty-four-track recorder was responsible for the horrible seventies tendency to pile lots of shit onto every track, and that beginning with *Another Green World* he was going to start experimenting with taking things away.

After *Surrender* I returned to my original path of getting there through a more traditional approach to liberating dissonance. To my mind this means not playing meaningless notes. But since all notes are potentially meaningful, we need to train ourselves to hear them as consonant rather than dissonant while playing with purpose and determination.

Mike: What's the freezer? Vermont?

Trey: All through 1996 we felt as though there was something new for us to discover about ourselves out there, but we didn't know what it was. And we were a little dissatisfied with having played more or less the same way for the past couple of years. And then suddenly our February Europe tour felt like a breakthrough. We were playing slow and funky, but in a distinctly Phish kind of way. I mean, we're not the Meters after all. And we kept it up throughout the whole summer tour and into the fall. Our second night in Denver [11/17/97], we felt, represented another breakthrough performance.

Fish: We always try to communicate with one another, even during the written sections. If Trey plays his part in a particularly inspired, aggressive, or subdued way, we respond to him. It establishes a mood, a unified emotional state that carries over into the jam.

Trey: We were drinking scotch at about four in the morning at an Italian truck stop during our first 1997 Europe tour when I heard this older guy yell, *"Vite, vite!* I saw you play in Milan! My friend wrote a book about Frank Zappa!" He dragged his friend over, who signed a copy of his book for me and talked all about Zappa this and Zappa that. All of a sudden I hear, "Frank Zappa! Phish! Frank Zappa!" from behind them. A five-man Zappa cover band who'd just finished a gig walked through the door and began to sing "City of Tiny Lights."

I have the highest respect for Zappa, for who he was, what he represented, and the fact that he didn't give a shit what anybody else thought about him or his music.

FRANK ZAPPA (1940–93) was many things at once: guitar hero, satirical songwriter, avant-garde composer, political gadfly, and cynical social commentator. He recorded more than sixty albums and played hundreds of shows in numerous different musical configurations. Zappa's life and work were tied together by what he referred to as a "conceptual continuity," in which every part was reflected in every other with holographic coherence. At the center of the hologram was the only person, he said, who could appreciate the totality of his work, namely Zappa himself.

As a composer, Zappa was influenced primarily by the twentieth-century composers Igor Stravinsky and Edgard Varèse. Zappa wrote, "Any composition (or improvisation) which remains *consonant* and '*regular*' throughout is, for me, equivalent to watching a movie with only '*good guys*' in it, or eating cottage cheese." As a performer and guitar hero, he was influenced by the sexual threat of protorocker Little Richard, the harmonica joys of fifties vocal groups such as the Velvets and the Robins, and the snarling blues guitar of Johnny "Guitar" Watson and Guitar Slim.

From *Freak Out* (1966) to *The Yellow Shark* (1993), and all the live work in between, all Zappa's music can be viewed together as a single, multifaceted, lifelong extended masterpiece of musical theater. Leaving no contemporary pop style untouched by his extreme notions of satire and parody, Zappa constantly evolved, extended, and revised his music with no goal beyond experiencing the continual pleasure of musical discovery. Phish, similarly, plays as though working on an ongoing composition in which the past is constantly revised in the present with an ear to the unheard.

OPPOSITE: Paradiso, Amsterdam, the Netherlands, February 17, 1997

Page: Zappa was never one of my favorites the way he was for Trey and Fish. I listened to a lot of stuff my older brother listened to, like the Beatles and Stones. I didn't really start listening to the Dead until college. Straight-ahead rock bands like the Who were much bigger influences on me than Zappa. My favorite Zappa album was *Hot Rats,* and "Peaches en Regalia," which we used to play a lot, was always my favorite song on it. Other than that, I never owned any of his albums. But I respect what he did and I'm glad he did it. It was always hard for me to get past his lyrics—a funny thing to say considering the band I'm in. And I'm not saying I'm above laughing at some Zappa lines, because I think a lot of them are pretty funny. Just don't expect to hear me say, "Hey, let's listen to that song about the poop chute!"

Fish: When drum magazines interview me, I usually say my favorite drummers are this guy, that guy, and all of Zappa's drummers. Aynsley Dunbar and Chester Thompson were more groove-oriented and a little looser than Terry Bozzio, who's more efficiently machinelike, with sharper edges. I like Vinnie Colaiuta a lot, too. I appreciate accuracy and tightness, but I also like to hear someone hang on to the back of the beat, play a little in front of it, or create space between the normal rests. But, at the same time, I always loved Yes drummer Bill Bruford, who's as close to a drum machine as a human being can get, and Buddy Rich, who's exacting and tight.

Zero Man backstage at the Somerville Theater, Somerville, Massachusetts, September 20, 1990

Trey: The Zappa drummers were some of Fish's biggest influences. I'm lucky to be in a band with a drummer who can play so many different styles, because most can only play one. Fish totally knocked me out from the minute I met him. We used to share a house in Burlington. He lived with his drum set in the pantry off the kitchen, right next to the garbage can. I'd stand in the kitchen writing music while he practiced. Every time he came up with a new groove, I'd write a song to fit it. I literally sat down and wrote "Lizards" on the other side of the door from him as he figured out how to play a calypso rhythm, with that high-hat upbeat. That takes a while, and he was at it for hours while I sat at the kitchen table with my guitar, tape deck, and a piece of paper.

Page: We all liked "Peaches en Regalia," and it was in *The Real Book* of jazz standards. We played a lot more jazz in 1986 and '87 than we do now, mainly because we had a regular gig for a couple of months as a jazz band with a horn player. We'd play standards all night. I was probably the impetus for the jazz direction, in the same way that Mike brought the bluegrass influence to the band, and everybody was happily into it. At the time, I was studying jazz with a Burlington piano player named Lar Duggan.

Trey: Zappa pushed his bands to the limit, wrote music that challenged people, and always worked at the edge of his abilities. A while ago I got my hands on some of his charts and discovered that his music consisted primarily of rhythmic explorations, while I wanted to work more in the harmonic domain. He was really into five-against-four rhythms and drone chords. Frank came from a modern classical background, and was greatly influenced by my favorite composer, Igor Stravinsky, who simply had it all.

In some songs I try to take listeners on a journey that ends in a different harmonic place than it began. "Horn," for example, starts off on a big E-major rock chord. My big gag is that I wrote a winding harmonic path far away from E that eventually resolves on E-flat. I wanted to fool the ear into thinking that E-flat was home, only home is really a half step lower, so it's a letdown. Pop music is all about expectation, and Barry Manilow goes for a whole-step rise in every fucking tune, which is something I've fought tooth and nail, because it's *so* predictable.

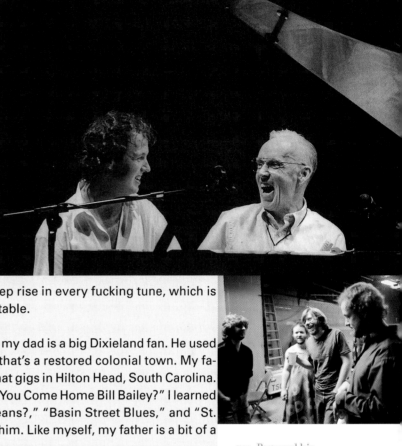

Page: I was exposed to a good bit of jazz as a child because my dad is a big Dixieland fan. He used to take me to JVC jazz fests in the part of Waterloo Village that's a restored colonial town. My father plays banjo and piano pretty well in a Dixieland band that gigs in Hilton Head, South Carolina. He's sung with us about three times. His big song is, "Won't You Come Home Bill Bailey?" I learned songs like "Do You Know What It Means to Miss New Orleans?," "Basin Street Blues," and "St. Louis Blues" on the piano at a fairly young age because of him. Like myself, my father is a bit of a ham and always wanted to be an entertainer.

I wasn't a prodigy, but my parents started taking me to piano lessons at four. I wanted to play guitar when I turned ten or so, but they kept me at it. I probably put up a real fight, so I give them a lot of credit for making me stick with it. There was a certain amount of parental concern when I announced my intention to be a professional musician—as well there should be when anyone decides to go into this business. But there was never a time when I didn't want to play professionally. I'm sure everybody has heard the line, "You need something to fall back on." But me, I didn't have anything to fall back on.

Trey: We started listening to tapes for the live album that became *Slip Stitch and Pass* around the time we were leaving on the summer USA tour. It takes three months after you hand in the fully completed album for the record company to release it. We were playing much better shows than that by the time it came out.

Page: I remember standing up and playing the clavinet in Hamburg during "Wolfman's Brother," with people basically sitting on the stage beside me, and thinking, "Man, this is really good." Mike was really grooving.

My attitude toward the way we play changed the most it ever had when I had to listen to tapes from our European tours in preparation for releasing *Slip Stitch and Pass*. I didn't want to release everything I heard, even from that Hamburg show, and I began to ask myself, "If it's not good enough to release, what the hell am I doing playing it live?"

TOP: Page and his father, Jack McConnell, Township Auditorium, Columbia, South Carolina, April 22, 1994
ABOVE: Backstage, Madison Square Garden, December 31, 1997

"THESE SONGS, PEOPLE UNDER-STAND THEM OR THEY CY ANN UNDERSTAND THEM, BUT Y'AVE FE SING THEM JUST THE SAME." —BOB MARLEY

CHANTING WORDS FROM A SONG: BEARSVILLE

IN NOVEMBER 1996, during their fall tour, Phish booked themselves into Seattle's Stepping Stone Studios and jammed for two days in the company of *Billy Breathes* producer Steve Lillywhite. One of the more successful musical experiments they performed there consisted of Lillywhite suggesting a familiar rock, funk, or soul song whose signature riff or vamp Phish would reproduce before veering off in a completely different direction.

After returning from Europe, Phish spent March 11 to 15 in Bearsville Studios outside of Woodstock, New York. The first of 1997's two Bearsville sessions consisted of agenda-free jams that combined *Surrender to the Air*'s unfettered spirit with the upgraded live chemistry they'd felt in Hamburg and elsewhere in Europe. Phish were eager to get back into the studio where, accompanied only by engineer John Siket, they hoped to maintain their onstage momentum. The band's goal was to translate their greatest strength—their jamming virtuosity—into successful songwriting. Page McConnell subsequently volunteered to sift through the resulting material for keepers.

OPPOSITE: Boiceville, New York, May 1996

Page: A week after the winter Europe tour we took the new sound that had been evolving into the Barn studio at Bearsville and jammed for four days straight, just making it up as we went along and really having fun. We'd always talked about going into the studio and getting good jams we could release, instead of just having good jams in the practice room or sound checks or even at gigs. We ended up with about twenty hours' worth of tape from that first session.

Trey: Any band member could kill a song at its first rehearsal if they wanted to. We constantly reexamine our roles and try to figure out ways to break out of them. That's why we switch instruments or all try to write things individually that we'll subsequently assemble into a song. Until going to Bearsville in March, we'd never gone into a studio with no material and just written together as a foursome with equal input.

Page: We ended up with material we could either use as basic tracks or even segues on the new studio album we began recording in April 1998. Whatever we don't use on that, I imagine, could eventually be released as an instrumental studio album.

THE DILEMMA most rock and pop bands face is how to translate their studio work to the stage. Phish has long had to deal with the opposite problem: how to capture their onstage energy in front of recording equipment rather than a live audience. Among the reasons for this is the schizoid nature of Anastasio compositions like "Divided Sky," "Reba," and "You Enjoy Myself"—songs their live shows could often hinge upon. All three songs begin with tightly composed sections that could be rehearsed and replayed in the studio until they were nailed; yet they all unfold into the sort of extended jams that can be glorious onstage but whose energy is less easily captured in the studio.

Mike: When we first played "Divided Sky" in the studio, I was reluctant to put it on a record because the jams had always sucked. I ended up enjoying the studio version because the bass and drums worked so well together. There have been times over the years when I didn't hold much affection for it, but lately I've really enjoyed playing it. It's hard to maintain affection for a song you've played six hundred times. Little Feat's "Six Feet of Snow," Rita Marley's "That's the Way," and the Grateful Dead's "Unbroken Chain," for example, are three of my favorite songs. They all have a chord built on the flat seven and a subtly implied key change cycling through them, which I love. But I prefer not to learn them, or even hear them that often, in order to retain the emotions they stir in me.

Trey: My mother has always written children's stories for a living. When I was in high school we wrote children's songs together as well as a musical called "Gus the Christmas Dog," which never went anywhere. The melodic middle part of "Divided Sky" came from something we wrote called "There's a Christmas Star," and the ending was the theme to "Gus." We had a whole dog motif going on. "If I Were a Dog" became the end of "Lizards." We also wrote songs for a kids' album called *Large Motor Skills*. We got paid about $250 a song. One of the things we wrote for the album went, "One fat walrus, two left shoes, three loud lions, and four cashews, five gooseberries, six old steaks, seven petunias, and eight big cakes."

Mike: In the "Mary Had a Little Lamb" section of "Divided Sky" Trey composed a guitar melody and we all made up lines to accompany it. Then we play it roughly backward, then forward again, when it segues into a Pat Metheny–ish section.

Page: We did a version of "Divided Sky" on the so-called "white tape" we recorded in the late eighties. But all the music after the "Ah, divided sky, the wind blows high" section came later.

Trey: "Divided Sky" was inspired by a night of mushroom consumption with Tom Marshall and Daubs [Marc Daubert] in the Princeton battlefield during our first year at Mercer Community College. The clouds inspired us to run around shouting the title. When I wrote the music to it, I was really into writing out different rhythm counts for each of us—and then making them all meet on the "one." You can work them out by saying "*ta ke gha malla,*" an Indian method of counting time I learned during a guitar lesson. The words break down measures of seven and eleven. To get all the different accents of a group of seven, for example, you can go "*ta ke ta ke gha malla,*" "*ta ke gha malla ta ke,*" or "*gha malla ta ke ta ke,*" which is a rhythm I used in "You Enjoy Myself."

"Divided Sky" and "You Enjoy Myself" were my first attempts to be really different, of trying to not conform to the traditional rules of songwriting. That makes them special to me. A lot of our old tunes were pieced together. "You Enjoy Myself" was written while Fish and I were busking in Europe. I wrote all the bits and pieces while we played street music for two months during the summer of 1984. The last thing I did before returning home was turn them into one big piece. "Fluffhead" is the big, obvious example of a song that was written as separate little pieces, then squished together.

"Reba" was the ultimate pieced-together tune. I wanted to get this compositional method out of my system, so I wrote each section based on the last note of the previous section. I put every idea on tape and then tried to forget it. The first time I heard the song all the way through was when I learned it piece by piece on guitar. "Reba" is structured like a fugue, which literally means "flight" or "chase," and every note counts. We work completely as a team for three straight minutes, then—*bam!*—we improvise. In "Reba" there's an echoing passage before the stops where every note Page plays echoes mine. During that time I'm hearing myself as one-fourth of a big sound, as opposed to strumming chords while Page takes a solo. I think it helps the jams, which become a release from complex compositional limitations, like being given your freedom. It's the opposite of, say, *Surrender to the Air*, where we start jamming from no context whatsoever.

The Barn, Bearsville Studios, May 1996

Fish: "Divided Sky" had long been one of our big bread-and-butter jam songs. But now "Down with Disease," "Simple," and even newer songs like "Ghost" have been stretching out more and taking the weight off the old workhorses we've gradually been putting out to pasture for a while.

Trey: You progress so long as you push your personal musical envelope, and I still enjoy some of the tunes I wrote long ago. As soon as I learned about modes, I tried to write one song in each of them. I wrote "Slave to the Traffic Light" as soon as I learned the open A-major chord. It's basically the same chord slid up and down the guitar neck, but so long as it's musical, who cares?

I wrote "The Landlady" during a great but frustrating Jazz in July workshop with Ted Dunbar at the University of Massachusetts. I really like the harmonic progression, especially in the B section. The A section is this II-V-I-to-minor thing similar to "Stash." The swing rhythm has always challenged us for a couple of reasons. First, if you're not swinging your whole life, you're not going to swing that well. Second, people dance to our music. Not that people didn't dance to swing bands. They sure did. But that kind of fast, beboppy, Charlie Parker style of swing is more for sitting, drinking, and listening to. It's tough to translate that into a big room.

Fish: We called it "The Landlady" because we imagined some angry landlady yelling at somebody while it was playing. I wish we played more swing, although it's hard to get away with it in arenas. "Magilla" sounds great in a club. And I lifted the high-hat and bass parts for "Stash" from Paul Motian's drumming on Bill Evans's version of "Green Dolphin Street."

ANASTASIO, frustrated by the conservative music program offered by the University of Vermont, transferred to Goddard College (as did Jon Fishman), where he was introduced to composer Ernie Stires by a mutual friend who rightly suspected that Stires had something to teach Trey. Stires, an escapee from the jingle-jungle advertising world, composes idiosyncratic music that often blends the melodic and improvisational pleasures of the big-band and swing music he grew up on with complex twentieth-century compositional techniques. The results are equally demanding and fun. "Trey looked like a drowned rat when he came over, but his musical sensibility seemed as freaky-deaky as mine was," recalls Stires. "He had a real affinity for the sort of atonal sonorities I go for, and some imaginative ideas he wanted to learn how to express. I tried to show him how to convey those ideas without destroying his interest in composing, and, I hope, served as a tonic for him when he desperately needed one." Anastasio returned the favor in 1997 by coproducing *Samson Riffs: The Music of Ernie Stires*, and by joining the pianist on the title track, a bopping jump duet.

Most of Anastasio's more complicated fugal works, which provided the tightly wound spring work for much of the band's improvising, were written during the late eighties and early nineties. After 1994's "Guyute," however, Anastasio drifted away from such pastiche-style compositions in order to explore other forms and techniques both traditional and new.

Trey: I wrote "Guyute," my most recent extended multipart composition, as an experiment in breaking some harmonic boundaries. In it each band member plays one step apart, which creates some heinous harmonies during the doubled-up sixteenth-note climbing section. The slow melody at the end is harmonized in a different wrong way. It suggests an obvious chord progression I changed completely. The lyrics describe a dream Tom had. I tried to make the music describe the lyric about an ugly pig scampering into the woods.

The first thing Ernie Stires taught me was, "If you're going to write music, you have to be able to play the piano." He handed me the music to Bach's "Well-Tempered Clavier," which contains forty-eight preludes and fugues in every major and minor key, and said, "Start at page one. Even if it takes you an hour to finger your way through the first two measures, do it. Just get from the beginning to the end like an inchworm. Play number two the next day and number three the day after that. When you finish the book, start over. When you finish it the second time, you'll be a piano player." I probably got through twelve of them, but it was enough to acquire some piano facility and comprehend the theory behind it, because Bach essentially invented harmony. I've always written music I can't play on piano. But I can pick through it enough to know how the harmony's going to sound. As Ernie said, "You're not training to perform on the piano. It's the composer's primary tool."

Ernie always said that the great timeless popular music, which for him would be the big-band era, was music in a three-and-a-half-minute format that could be enjoyed by everyone, on all levels. You could dance to it, listen to the singer or melody, get into the solos, dissect the arrangement, or simply dig the groove. It was all there, in one tidy package.

OPPOSITE: Trey and Ernie Stires at Ernie's house, Cornwall, Vermont ABOVE: Bearsville Studios, May 1996

Page: Each tour I'll forget a part of one of our more complicated, worked-out songs, like "Divided Sky" or "You Enjoy Myself," and I'll have to go back and relearn it. It's just a brain fart, one note or a little passage I space out on. I'll usually try to relearn the whole thing, to make sure I'm learning it correctly rather than glossing over parts. Each song gets a going-over every few years.

Trey: For years we were completely ignored by the world at large. Then in 1992 *People* magazine, in our first piece of national press, voted *A Picture of Nectar* one of the ten worst albums of the year. Suddenly there we were, next to Madonna and Bobby Brown. A guy stopped me on the street and said, "I saw you in *People* magazine. I figured if they hated it that much, I'd probably love it. So I bought your album."

ANASTASIO'S earlier music was often hung on fantasy lyrics that told quirky stories. The most ambitious of these was "The Man Who Stepped into Yesterday," known to fans simply as "Gamehendge," which Anastasio wrote to fulfill his senior project requirement at Goddard. Gamehendge's beginnings lie in the Anastasio/Woolfe/Marshall song "Wilson" and in Tom Marshall's poem "McGrupp and the Watchful Hosemasters." "The Man Who Stepped into Yesterday" has assumed mythical significance among Phish fans over the years. The band has

only performed it onstage four times, and its familiarity among audience members is largely due to widely circulated tapes of the piece Anastasio and his bandmates recorded in 1988 to fulfill his course requirement. Ambitious, stylistically varied, full of loose wordplay and the short-attention-span fables of a natural storyteller, "The Man Who Stepped into Yesterday" and songs like "Fee," "Esther," and "Fluff's Travels" are oddball inventions indeed.

Trey: What I most enjoy about writing lyrics is making up stories, like the ones I occasionally tell onstage. I got on a roll with "The Man Who Stepped into Yesterday" because I was writing a lot of music at the time and it gave me something to write about. I'm kind of a workaholic and really like moving forward. I was into words, sounds, and stories, but nothing particularly personal. I was probably influenced most by Genesis's *The Lamb Lies Down on Broadway,* which I was obsessed with in high school. I wrote "The Man Who Stepped" while living in a crappy little basement apartment of a condemned building near a river. One day I discovered that my sink emptied directly into a crawl space underneath the floor, and I was apparently feeding the entire river-rat population of Plainfield, Vermont. I could hear them scampering in the wall right beside my ear all night long. One night I saw one run across my bed, which was a futon on the floor.

Even after finishing "Gamehendge" I could get into a song's music without having to worry too much about content because I'd already established a cast of characters. So a song like "Punch You in the Eye," for example, was a lot easier to write than it might have been because I didn't have to write about myself. And its first line—"I come from the land where the oceans freeze"—was inspired by a visit with my mother, who at the time lived in an Irish town where people would swim in the freezing ocean every Christmas.

Mike: I've always rebelled against the Gamehendge thing. I like the idea of our having an unexplained and uncapitalized-upon mythology, but I never related to it personally. The story's moral, that the revolutionary will eventually turn into another evil Wilson, always felt predictable and not all that clever to me, so I never internalized it. I was always against recording an electric Gamehendge album, but I got pretty psyched about doing an acoustic version because I've enjoyed playing all the Gamehendge songs at different times. On the other hand, I haven't always been a big fan of musicals, whereas Trey's mother took him to many Broadway shows.

Trey: We've received offers from film companies to do animated versions of "Gamehendge," and it could still happen. But I always prefer doing new things, and Mike especially has always shied away from doing it onstage because he considers it more me than Phish.

The thing about "Gamehendge" that gets lost sometimes is that it's full of jokes, beginning with the name itself. And while the whole rock-opera concept bugs and embarrasses me on a certain level, "The Man Who Stepped into Yesterday" is a pretty good one. It contains some interesting musical ideas, like the descending chromatic line runs that run through the "Lizards" chord progression before it ascends and goes into the calypso groove, the weird harmonies in "Tela," and "Colonel Forbin's Ascent," which is full of rich jazz chords, dissonant notes, and interesting internal lines you probably don't hear very well on the electric guitar.

Page: "Axilla" might be the last Gamehendge song ever written. I don't get much of it, but it was an answer in the crossword puzzle I did last night. The clue was "Pertaining to the armpit," and the answer was "axillial," which I wouldn't have known if I hadn't been in this band. I don't think of armpits when I sing it, naturally.

Trey: We learned "The Man Who Stepped into Yesterday" and recorded it in our living room as quickly as possible. We recorded it onto one cassette, bounced it to another, and added the lyrics on top so the words come out of one speaker and the music out of the other. I've always felt as though it were an unfinished project in a way, because we decided to record what became *Junta* rather than develop Gamehendge fully.

What you don't get when it's performed live is all the scored music performed underneath the narration, although some of it, like those little descending bass lines, got recycled in tunes like "Esther." The original idea was to have a really old narrator, possibly an elderly woman, and compose fully orchestrated segues between songs sung by vocalists other than ourselves, with different instrumentation.

WHEN HE'S NOT holed up in a Vermont farmhouse writing songs with Anastasio, or getting himself thrown out of the band room on tour, Tom Marshall is a software-tweaking professional who seems most comfortable outside the Phish spotlight despite having contributed essential components of the band's identity. Marshall's words balance Anastasio's bright compositional yang with dank verbal yin that often urges the music into darker and more emotionally compli-

cated spaces. Marshall, working in a genre diluted by a million silly, sad, angry, or syrupy love ditties, writes open-ended songs that transcend you-me-us clichés and suggest as many meanings as there are pairs of ears to hear them. Lines like these from "Limb by Limb"—"Lingering slowly and melting away / Tossed with the salad and baled with the hay / Pooling like water that drips from above / Trampled by lambs and pecked by the dove"— describe equally well a dissolving relationship as well as the ego fragmentation concertgoers may experience at Phish shows during those moments when the music seems to come untied from its moorings and dissolve into nothingness. With its superimposed rhythms and feeling of heavily stressed machinery on the verge of exploding into lethal fragments, "Limb by Limb" sounds like a band taking itself apart, and then reassembling, every time it's played.

Fish: We've all contributed songs over the years, but only two of us are very active. One's so prolific it's ridiculous. The other one, Mike, tends to hoard stuff away until it's more fully developed. Trey's nervier, and brings things to us in a much rawer form than Mike, who tends to deliver the best of what he's saved up. The band has recorded only four of my songs, on four different albums, and each one was a nerve-wracking experience. My songwriting career began in 1984, when I bought a little $25 acoustic guitar to keep me busy while I hitchhiked in Alaska. It really came in handy when I spent forty-eight hours waiting for a ride. The first thing I wrote was the Jimmy-your-cat-died thing in "Harpua."

Trey: I remember stupid little songs about my cat running away that I wrote in the third or fourth grades. In school, I must have written a thousand tunes with Tom and our friends. That was our social life: a bunch of guys hanging out and writing tunes. We'd even go to parties and immediately convene in the back room to make up songs. My acquiring a four-track tape deck took everything to another level.

Tom Marshall: Writing for Phish is really the high point of my existence. Aaron and I wrote the song that became "Wilson" for our band A-Dot Tom with the sole purpose of making ourselves burst into hysterics whenever we "performed" it. Aaron wrote, "Out near Stonehenge, I live alone." I added, "Out near Gamehendge, I chafed a bone," and we took it from there. We sang it to several people one night at a party at our friend Roger's house, and they all laughed at it. Then we sang it to Trey, who had a completely different reaction.

Trey: Most of those guys continued to write songs together at PDS, but I left. In '83 I bumped into Tom and Daubs again at Mercer County Community College, which strongly resembled the New Jersey Department of Motor Vehicles. I still don't know what the hell we were doing there, but Phish had been together for about six months at this point and I was taking a math class. One day I bumped into Tom and said, "Come hang out at my house." We ended up starting a band and over the next couple of months recorded a tape called *Bivouac Jaun,* sixty minutes of the two of us alternating lines of poetry and falling over in hysterics. I only made four copies of it, and three of them are lost.

Tom: Trey can write around lyrics better than anyone I know. He makes the music fit them perfectly, sometimes on purpose and sometimes unconsciously. For years I'd typically fax Trey ten poems, and he'd turn them into a single song. He's more of an editor than a lyrical collaborator. He'll suggest an alternative line, a better way to sing it, or cut something out. He always calls to ask if it's okay to move things around, and I always say yes. Turning a poem into a song is a type of creative rebirth, like transforming a two-dimensional picture into a three-dimensional object. My favorite thing in the world is coming home from work and finding a new Trey song using my words on my answering machine. It's an incredibly cool thing.

Bearsville Studios, May 1996

Trey: "Run Like an Antelope" appeared first on the *Bivouac Jaun* tape. I had a four-track recording studio and a piano. The breezy first section of "Antelope" consisted of odd little sound effects; next came the big E-minor/D-minor jam, with a brief reggae section at the end. I just pieced together whatever I was working on in the sequence I wrote it. My friend Steve Pollak, the Dude of Life, is an incredibly creative guy bursting with great song concepts. About a week before I wrote this music in my basement, Steve had told me there should be a song with the chorus, "Set the gearshift for the high gear of your soul. You've got to run like an antelope out of control." So I stuck it in there. The rest of the words were a complete afterthought, but they gave Tom Marshall his big break. I held up the microphone to him as he walked into our basement and he said, "Rye rye rocco. Marco Esquandolas."

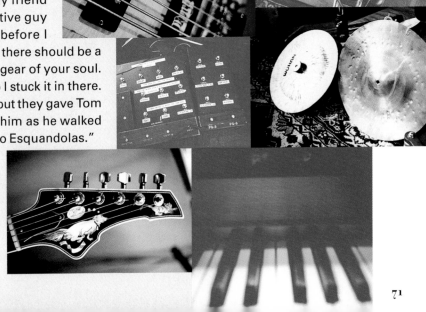

Mike: To be brutally honest, I don't know a lot of our lyrics. I hope I know the ones I sing, but I don't sing most of them. I should concentrate on the words more than I do, but most of the time I'm thinking

groove. Certain words seep through as "emotional triggers" for me. I read a psychology paper a while back that showed how certain words, guitar riffs, and other elements of acid rock become a murky pile of emotional triggers. It said that someone on acid will appreciate all the little pieces of psychedelic music while simultaneously believing it all points to emptiness, like Zen Buddhism. I can relate to that feeling. Our lyrics contain many emotional triggers for me: feelings, a specific memory, or a sentimental rush. And much of the time I'm only thinking about the bass line.

Trey: Tom and I had a lyrical hump to get over after *A Picture of Nectar*. Some of its lyrics are still really funny, and it had "Chalk Dust" on it, but it was mainly a "Cavern" vibe. So *Rift* was a reaction to *Nectar* because I didn't want to be boxed in.

Tom: I'm horribly embarrassed by the lyrics to "Stash." I enjoy the way they're sung, but as far as meaning goes, they're value-free. When people ask me what they mean, I always say, "Work it out for yourself." Except for *Billy Breathes,* I don't think you could immediately become a Phish fan without doing a little work.

Trey: Zappa asked if humor belonged in music. Yeah, it does. But a better question for Zappa might have been, Is humor the *only* thing that belongs in music? You have to be careful about that, too.

Tom: Somebody once asked me if it affects how I write to realize it could be a hit single or something. But I'm really only writing for my friend Scott Herman, who sees all my poems before anyone else does. I e-mail him everything I write. Sometimes he just acknowledges receiving them, sometimes he adds lines or makes revisions, and sometimes he doesn't respond at all.

Trey: It's a struggle for Phish to write songs together. Before leaving for Europe, though, we said, "Damn it, we're gonna write together no matter how it comes out." So we wrote "Walfredo," "Rock-a-William," and "Carini Had a Lumpy Head," which were okay. Then we tried to solve the problem another way by going into Bearsville after the Europe tour with no songs whatsoever. Even though I had new songs with Tom, I didn't play them for the guys and we started recording from degree zero. The plan was to edit it together and then come up with lyrics afterward.

A lot of people—both friends and relatives—send me lyrics now. But Tom's are nearly always the only ones I can sing. I completely make his voice my own.

Page: We switched instruments onstage during the fall '95 tour, first in Hampton, Virginia [11/25/95], then again in Philadelphia [12/15/95]. The idea started out as a joke. We were going to learn a Led Zeppelin song we'd play while switching instruments in rotation. Each of us would have to learn the same song on four instruments. In the end we decided to just jam and see what happens. Eventually we ended up writing "Walfredo" and "Rock-a-William" as songs to play on instruments other than our own.

A view of Trey from the control room, Bearsville Studios, May 1996

Tom: Simple lyrics are so much better than weirdness for its own sake. I grew up on Pink Floyd, King Crimson, and Genesis, but now I prefer the Rolling Stones, Bob Dylan, and Neil Young.

Trey: Where are the great lyrics of today? Turn on the radio. Most of what you hear is pretentious, idiotic, posed shit, and people buy right into it.

Tom: Despite whatever the lyrics happen to say, Trey's music determines the mood of any particular song. When I gave him the lyrics to "Sparkle" and "Horn," he said, "This is the most depressing stuff I've ever read. I'm going to make 'Sparkle' a happy song." So it always cracks me up to see the audience dancing and laughing and ignoring the falling-apart part. And I love the introspective jam at the end of "Horn."

Mike: "Sparkle" can cheer me up if I'm in a bad mood. Even if it doesn't hold any surprises, I like watching the room moving underneath Chris's circling lights. I usually don't notice the lights because my eyes are closed.

Tom: "The pressure builds / You buy a gift / You're hoping that your dread will lift." This was when I felt extremely pressured to get married. It's one of the few songs my wife knows is about her.

Trey: Mike once told me that bluegrass music often combines sad lyrics with happy music. Shortly thereafter I received a pile of poems from Tom. I saw "Sparkle" and thought, "Wow! These are really sad lyrics. Let's write a bluegrass tune." A lot of listeners probably think the final line is "laugh and laugh and fall apart" rather than "laugh and laughing fall apart," which is something very different. You never want to lose your sense of humor, even in the worst situation. I've always wondered what I'd do in a plane crash, for example, but what I'd *like* to do is call Fish's answering machine and say, "I finally figured it out! The meaning of life is . . ."

Page: The nice thing about "Sparkle" is that we can fall apart rhythmically at the end of the song, and it still works just fine.

Tom: I never knew "Chalk Dust Torture" would become a rock song. It had more of a moody I-hate-school feeling when I wrote it. When I gave it to Trey, I was mainly curious as to how he'd handle the five-line verses.

Engineer Jon Siket
(FAR LEFT) and the
band at Studio A,
Bearsville Studios,
October 1997

Bearsville Studios,
May 1996

Trey: "Chalk Dust" is about some kid gazing out the window imagining this insane roller-coaster jam. It makes me think about Mozart, and the fact that his father gave him the tools he needed so he could write music as fast as he could think it. A lot of kids out there probably have the talent and imagination but lack the tools.

Fish: "Chalk Dust" grew on me like a fungus. It rose from literally being my least favorite song, a song I hated, to becoming my favorite song for a while. On a good night, the sky's the limit. It's as straight as a rock song can get, and I love the whole live-while-you-can thing. I want to still be playing "Chalk Dust" when I'm eighty, crying, "Can I live while I'm young?" The older we get, the more desperate it sounds, which is great.

Mike: "Chalk Dust" is a good song to zone out to; the frantic energy acts like a gateway to a dream. It blares and stomps, but at the same time you can sink back and meditate on it.

Page: We've historically been pretty good at playing weird grooves in odd time signatures. The simpler straight-ahead stuff has not been our forte, so we've tried to concentrate on it during the past few years. Now "Chalk Dust" feels as comfortable as anything else we play, and while it was never intended as a rock anthem, it certainly became one.

Tom: "Chalk Dust Torture" was one of the last songs I wrote on paper prior to discovering the computer as my main compositional tool. I get a lot of songwriting done when I should be working.

Mike: It's good to have rock songs, to be a regular rock band.

Trey: When I record demos with Tom, I'm never inclined to pick up a guitar until we get rolling; before that, it's all about singing and arrangements. I play a lot of piano, drums, and bass, which are the important songwriting instruments for me, with the guitar always an afterthought. I guess I'm a guitarist with Phish because the bass and drums are taken care of.

Tom's the "Jersey drunk" on tour, the guy who drinks all the beer backstage. But he's a major creative force in my life, and everything this band has accomplished from the very beginning has been influenced immensely by his sense of humor. Not to mention that Aaron Woolfe and he were my songwriting heroes in ninth grade.

Tom has an incredible sense of language and wordplay. He has an extreme personality, and whatever stage of life he's going through comes out in his lyrics with almost brutal honesty. I try to grab lines from his poetry that mean something different to me than they do to him, figuring if they mean something different to me, they mean something different to other people too.

Page: Going through and listening to everything we recorded in Bearsville seemed almost overwhelming, so nobody really did it right away. The band spent some time apart right after that.

I went to Asia, Trey had another baby, and when we returned, Trey had listened to our Europe tapes and put together *Slip Stitch and Pass.* So I volunteered to go through all our Bearsville tapes.

What jumped out at me from the first Bearsville sessions was how many tracks had the structure and feel of complete songs, with A and B sections. It seemed we were consciously, or unconsciously, creating music we could cut into songs, complete with melodies and chord progressions. We ended up with at least half a dozen pieces from seven to ten minutes long that really worked as complete thoughts.

Trey: Sometimes I'll think some new song can be our next something-or-other, but that's always a dead end. "Maze" will never be the next "David Bowie" or whatever, and it's still developing its own personality. In "Maze" I sometimes get a hint of us playing the way Mike's mother, Marge Minkin, paints. She does big swooshes of color on huge pieces of canvas. "Maze" is moving slowly in that direction.

I've written many songs because we needed something for the set list. I want us to have songs in every key, major and minor jams in every mode, and something for each band member to sing. The fact that I always wrote for the stage might explain why our album career has always lagged behind our live career. I'll think, "We could use a rocking set closer," then write something like "Character Zero." At one point I wanted something with a blues progression and doubled-up rhythm; we were playing with the Aquarium Rescue Unit, and they played lots of fast tunes. So I wrote "Llama" on tour while we were staying at Page's parents' house.

Page: Among the tunes we came up with in Bearsville is "The Happy Whippin' Dung Song"— imagine driving through a blinding snowstorm in the tundra with a yak, a sled, and a heaving pile of steaming dung—"Cataract Man," and "The Meatstick," which we added lyrics to in Vienna with Tom one night after we'd cleaned out the minibar and only the beef sticks remained. It has a dance, too, but you won't see me doing it.

Trey: Working with Tom is the purest form of collaboration I've ever experienced next to jamming onstage with Phish at its best. We don't even have to talk anymore, we just go right to it. There's no baggage or turf to worry about. If I add a line, it's okay. Or Tom might come to the table with an A section, I'll immediately come up with a B section, and he'll supply the words. We've gotten to the point where he'll walk into the room, I'll stick the microphone in his face, and he'll sing the right line. After all, we've been working on our songwriting partnership even longer than Phish has its jamming relationship.

Page: Going to Bearsville ended up being a fairly involved process, which is why we've only done it twice and probably won't do it again for a while. First, it ain't cheap to record at Bearsville. We spent tens of thousands of dollars during the eight days we spent there this year. Second, it's a lot harder than you might imagine to wade through everything we recorded.

I found the stuff from the first session to be really special in a way the second session wasn't. It had to do with our attitude going in after having played Hamburg a week before. We were all on the verge of, "Oh my God! It's all out there, anything we want!" Thank gosh we went in when we did, because we would have missed that unique snapshot of what the band could do at the studio when left to our own devices for four days.

TAKEN FAR AWAY: EUROPE REPRISE

UPON RETURNING from Bearsville, Phish played a rare hometown gig in Burlington's handsome Flynn Theater, on March 18. A benefit for Lake Champlain environmental efforts, the Flynn show also marked the debut of Ben & Jerry's Phish Food ice cream. The band also contributes its share of the proceeds from this seductive chocolate, caramel, and natural-marshmallow concoction to the restoration of Lake Champlain.

After rehearsing new material, Phish returned to Europe, where they played nineteen dates between June 13 and July 11. In addition to their debut performance at the Royal Albert Hall in London, the band played five music festivals, including the venerable Roskilde Festival in Denmark and England's Glastonbury Festival, Phish's first opportunity to wail the familiar "Wilson" lyric—"Oh, out near Stonehenge, I lived alone"—within earshot of the stony site itself. Other notable moments included a lengthy karaoke sound check/limbo contest in Genova, Italy, and a second-set jam session with Bela Fleck and his band in Lyon, France.

As set lists began to filter back, older crowd pleasers such as "Suzy Greenberg" and "Golgi Apparatus," as well as jam warhorses like "Tweezer" and "David Bowie," appeared to be missing in action. On the other hand, the band debuted more than a dozen new songs—including "Ghost," "Twist," "Dirt," and "I Saw It Again"—during the two Dublin shows that began the tour.

Phish use set lists as yet another compositional element in their artistic gestalt. Written mainly by Anastasio, with input from the other band members, the set lists traditionally have taken several factors into consideration. Where is the band playing? Is it a single show or part of a multishow run? What material did they play here last time? What's new? What songs haven't made it into the rotation lately? From the point of view of fans, set lists are fetish objects, the jam-rock equivalent of British train spotting.

OPPOSITE: Fleet Center, Boston, Massachusetts, December 31, 1996

Road manager Brad Sands used to photocopy Anastasio's set lists for Chris Kuroda, Paul Languedoc, and the band. "Sometimes Trey wouldn't have anything planned until five minutes before the set was supposed to begin. So if the break's already been half an hour, and I have to make copies and tape them down, it could really drag on." Even then, "half the time they'd give the set list to me and Paul and the first song would be different," Kuroda says. "They literally wouldn't play a song from the list we just got. It's not intentional. They'd get up there, feel some vibe, and, you know, things change."

Page: We made a few conscious decisions before going on our second European tour in June. Mainly we decided to take a look at our song list, which became a vehicle for us to reconsider everything we were doing. So during band practices leading up to the tour we actually voted on which songs we wanted to play and which ones we wanted to ditch. We asked ourselves what material was making us happy and genuinely exciting us. Because they're all great songs in their own ways, and each has had its little moment or two, but it doesn't mean that every one of them is exactly where we are now.

Fish: For better or worse, bands that remain together a long time acquire a signature sound. One of the ways we try to avoid getting stale is by treating each song as a fifth personality in the band and honoring it as an independent entity. Each of our songs has its own personality, its particular strengths and weaknesses, and a capacity for exploration you may or may not be immediately aware of.

Talking with lighting director Chris Kuroda (RIGHT), Fleet Center, December 31, 1996

Page: We trimmed our song list in light of Trey and Tom's having rented a farmhouse in Stowe and written a whole slew of good new songs we learned between the two Europe tours. So we got rid of an equal number of tunes we'd decided we weren't going to play in Europe and over the summer, at least until the Great Went. Our new goals consisted of getting comfortable with the fresh material, and serious jamming.

Fish: We ended up editing about fourteen songs from our song list—anything three band members didn't want to play anymore got cut. We cleared the air of a bunch of tunes we thought we were sick of playing. I relate to songs in much the same way I relate to people. I get tired of being around the same person in the same context all the time. Meanwhile, certain songs had become crutches to elicit reactions from the crowd. We knew the crowd would go *wooo* whenever we played "Suzy Greenberg," and it got boring and felt manipulative. I love communicating with our audience and working it into a wild frenzy, but I prefer earning that frenzy the hard way.

When Trey used to write set lists, he felt compelled to organize a big show that represents a little of everything we do, as opposed to just going onstage and seeing what happens. He wanted some piano, some vocals, some instrumentals, some places for us to stretch out, and some nice arrangements. "Flow" and "variety" were his watchwords. But when we hit those European clubs, we really dug our heels in and played in a more relaxed manner than we ever had before. The crowds were older, too, so we leaned toward more substantial music.

Trey: I once made a list of all our songs at the time. One category was Big Jams; another was Worked Out, except I mistakenly wrote "Woked Out." I ended up not being able to decide which category to put a lot of our songs in. It was a nice idea, but I guess it didn't woke out.

Page: The editing process was an important and effective way for us to seriously consider what we were communicating. Ironically, we've already brought back almost everything we said we weren't going to play anymore. It was more about what we sing than what we play. Some of our songs, like "Dinner and a Movie," are just one-line jokes that have worn thin over time. I wanted to ax fewer tunes than other band members, but everyone was happy to get rid of "Suzy." It's not that it isn't a great little ditty and a pop classic in its own right, but it just doesn't do it for us anymore. I want to reach the point where the groove is at a religious level nearly all the time, and not be distracted by joke songs. Because that's what our audience and the rest of the band really want, too.

Fish: We cut "Golgi Apparatus," "Suzy Greenberg," "Wilson," "Weigh," "Tweezer," and "Contact," among others. I can play "Contact" until the cows come home, but Mike was sick of singing it. Typically, I wielded the heaviest ax by far. I circled all the big jam songs, our very bread and butter, in hopes of forcing us to come up with new jam springboards. Not too long after this, though, we opened our Glastonbury, England, set with "Wilson" because Stonehenge was only two miles away, and when would the song's first line ever be more relevant?

Just about every song we do becomes my favorite at some point, usually during its early stages. I loved "Split Open and Melt" at first, then became bored with it, and then fell in love with it again after the major breakthrough with it that ended up at the end of "Demand" on *Hoist* [4/21/93]. All our songs have unique life cycles. It's like having lots of kids, because they all contain elements of the band and its various personalities. The songs we play at any given time reflect our collective internal state.

Trey: I'm basically sick of "Suzy Greenberg." We've been playing it so long that it doesn't mean anything anymore. But that funky three-chord groove sure can be fun to jam over.

Fish: I like "Suzy"'s music but I don't think the lyrics reflect any of us. It's basically a misogynist rejection song about some chick who turned Steve Pollak down years ago. It was funny for a while, and it was always a perfect song for horns.

SOME OF PHISH'S most popular songs—including "Fluffhead," "Suzy Greenberg," and "Sanity"—were written or cowritten by Steve Pollak, otherwise known as the Dude of Life. Anastasio befriended Pollak in high school, where they played together in the band Space Antelope. Edgier than Anastasio's solo compositions, the Anastasio/Dude collaborations contain less interpretive space than the guitarist's later collaborations with Tom Marshall.

"At the time 'Fluffhead' was written," the Dude recalls, "my oldest brother was dying of cancer. He passed away in 1983, when Trey and I were both attending the University of Vermont. At a Dead show, we saw a guy in the crowd, obviously a cancer patient himself, who had fluff balls on his head. We wrote the song about that guy in the crowd, but looking back I realize it's really about my brother."

How did the Dude become the Dude? "That goes back to when Trey and I were going to the Taft School," he says. "It was late one night when everyone had taken mushrooms. I walked into the room clad in tapestry, goggles, and a hat, and started uttering certain wisdoms." Such as? "I haven't the slightest idea. But the next thing I knew, I was knighted the Dude of Life, and I've been the Dude of Life ever since."

Phish recorded the album *Crimes of the Mind* with the Dude in 1991, and have performed with him and his rubber chickens onstage many times. Released by Elektra in 1994, *Crimes* suggests where Phish might have gone as a somewhat more mainstream rock band exuding raw energy. "Today Phish is an empire," says the Dude. "Back then we were just a bunch of stoned college kids."

Pursuing his solo career in the New York City area, with a new album in the works, the Dude abides.

Page: I want to perform an entire show without feeling embarrassed about having to sing one line or another. That feels like maturity to me, and it helps the jamming stay focused as well.

Trey: I always think about turning old songs that are threatening to go stale upside-down. For example, I'd like to start the "Antelope" jam at the top and work down. Or play "Maze" really slow. Of course if I really had my way, I'd write all new material.

Mike: The Dude of Life wrote a few other songs we don't play anymore, such as "Fluorescent Gerbils," which first evolved into "Skippy the Wonder Mouse" and then into "McGrupp and the Watchful Hosemasters," which became part of the Gamehendge mythology.

Trey: After we collaborated at UVM, he transferred to SUNY Purchase in New York. Down there he wrote all these great songs that ended up on *Crimes of the Mind*. The coolest thing about *Crimes* was the pressure was off us; it wasn't a Phish album. It was arranged and recorded quickly, and it still sounds fresh to me. I love the buildup in "TV Show," the outro to "Swiss Miss Girl," and some of our weird crossing harmonies. Sometimes I think we would have been a great backup band, because we don't have a real front person. Really, it's just incredible playing with Steve. He's a natural-born entertainer and one of the funniest and most genuine people I've ever met.

Page: This guy came out wearing a gas mask and running around like a wild man the first time we played Johnson State College. It was the Dude of Life, who I'd heard about for ages but had never met. He sang "Suzy Greenberg" and it was great. He's a talented and funny guy, with a knack for writing catchy songs, but most of the times we've played with him it hasn't worked that well for me. It's like seeing another act in the middle of our show. When he gets onstage, he wants to be completely out front, working the crowd, which comes naturally to him. He's a friend of Trey's, though, so the last time he wanted to play with us I ended up making the dreaded "call from Page" you don't want to get when you're in the Phish organization. I'm not that hard a guy. I just don't have a problem doing what's best for the band.

Trey: "Punch You in the Eye" was written just to hear the Nectar's audience yell for it. In those days I personally knew everyone in the club. Remember all those people yelling during "Icculus" on *Junta*? I know who they all are. We'd play our set and Rob Desaro would drunkenly scream "Punch me in the eye! Punch me in the eye!" the entire night. I always liked the idea of somebody walking in off the street into this surreal scene. That was the idea behind the secret language, too, when everybody is supposed to suddenly fall to the ground, turn around, or yell "D'oh!" I always imagined someone wandering into a show, not knowing what's going on, and everyone around them suddenly disappearing.

WITH THEIR TRAMPOLINES, secret language, Big Ball Jams, a drummer in a dress, and songs about girls deserving neurological examinations, a reputation as a joke band sometimes preceded Phish in the greater rock marketplace. For Phish, however, these were only amusing distractions in lengthy shows worthy of comic relief. The trampolines actually goofed on the choreographed guitar routines seen in heavy metal bands like Poison, and in fact established Phish as the world's first acrobatic acid rockers. And the ninety-nine versions of the Big Ball Jam Phish performed between November 1992 and December 1994—consisting of each band member improvising in sync with one of four inflated balls tossed around by the audience—were a form of inspired musical chaos that let the crowd "play the band," and in doing so acknowledged the audience's contribution to the event.

Page: We decided to play "Highway to Hell" as an encore to one of the best shows of the fall '96 tour, at UCLA. It wasn't bad, but it went too far. It felt like a wasted opportunity or a joke you were sick of hearing. Our big gags usually tend to come off, however. We did a gig in Lille, France, this tour, where Fish got out a folding chair, drummed on a pillow in his lap, and sang Paul Simon's "Cecilia" without knowing most of the words. It was a silly and stupid Fish kind of thing, and it was a riot. Every once in a while it feels appropriate to loosen up and play our goofier stuff. Plenty of nights we've gotten Fish out there to sing, and I'd think, "Damn, why didn't we play a real song?" We're not doing the Fish solo stuff as much as we used to, yet Fish is singing ten times more than he did before—real songs. His vocals used to be a joke. Now he's singing a lot of four-part harmonies with us. He's got a good voice, too.

THE LANGUAGE

Chinese	–	basic alert
hi trill	–	attention
tritone **down**	–	½ speed, speed up (2x speed if tritone up)
½ step down	–	go down ½, up whole, down ½
popeye	–	Ambient Bb
Circus	–	sing a note
simpsons	–	doe
weep, weep, weep	–	Waltz on to G
I let a song	–	go to specified new song
Get back	–	return to 1st song of series, or prev.
Sound of Silence	–	silence (don't play on it), fake "blip"
Will the Circle	–	do cycle of fourths (at rate of organ)
If it aint got swing	–	swing
Scraping	–	"oh fuck!"
Up Up Away, hi note	–	start at top go down (arhythmic if hi note a vibrato)
Up Up Away, lo note	–	start at bottom, go up
raising ½ steps	–	laugh
raising ½ steps/lo note	–	ha, ha, ha, blup
Me & My arrow	–	point at a person
hi note	–	tall person
same note	–	normal person
lo note	–	short person
slo vibrato	–	
fast vibrato	–	
star trek	–	wesley
close song	–	geezer
ask jerry	–	asshole
tritone	–	give them finger

Lawn Boy photo session, Boston, 1990

Fish: I first played the vacuum cleaner as a dare. One night at a party I was bragging that not only could I play any instrument, I taught the other band members how to play *their* instruments. Sofi Dillof pointed to a vacuum cleaner and said, "Here, big shot. Can you play *this*?" I turned it on, stuck it in my face, and immediately realized that, depending on the size of your mouth hole, a vacuum hose indeed makes a wild assortment of sounds as it sucks in your face. My first thought was, "Wow, any idiot could do this"—and probably many idiots have. The difference between me and those other idiots, however, is that I have a stage to do it on. My next thought was that having discovered this, I definitely had to use it at our next gig to establish myself as a vacuum virtuoso, which I did.

My only advice to anyone wanting to play the vacuum would be not to—because I've done it, and you'd only be ripping me off. And if you're not careful, it can rip apart your gums and teeth. I have an image of myself as an old man with one side of my face nice and firm and the other just one long jowl. If you pull the air over your lips, it makes a whistling sound, and I've played a couple of melodies that way. If I practiced, I could probably learn scales on the damn thing. But I've never practiced it, so it's hit or miss. It's really just a glorified farting machine, and now it's up to somebody else to take it to the next level.

As far as axes go, I started out playing a 1962 Electrolux canister, but it died. The '56 I replaced it with has hung in there just fine.

Page: The vacuum cleaner, the silent jams, standing frozen still, the dances, trampolines, big balls, secret language—the jokes and gimmicks come and go, but I've enjoyed them all.

Trey: We headed back to Europe wanting our new songs to be the shows' high points, which began to happen. And suddenly those old songs we'd stopped playing felt fresh again. For example, people were probably getting sick of hearing "Squirming Coil" two or three years ago, because I really liked calling for it. But I began to miss it this summer and just loved it when we ended up playing it once or twice toward the end of the year.

Fish: In Europe we learned to play even faster by expending a lot less energy. Part of it was a mental economy of motion. Music suddenly became easier when we simply embraced the traditional roles of our respective instruments.

We've never been the sort of band where everyone just vamped underneath a soloist; there's always a conversation going on underneath whoever's soloing. If somebody is having a particularly rich flow of ideas, then obviously he's the guy to pass the ball to. But more and more often it's as though the three other band members add up to a single multifaceted instrument I'm playing either off of or in conjunction with. And when I'm playing my best, it's as though I'm playing off what all *four* of us are doing. It's literally as though I were hovering above the band and observing myself playing all the instruments simultaneously from my drum set, and I feel it's all a result of paying attention.

Trey: We learned a couple of Meters tunes in band practice as an exercise in slowing down our back beat. We'd learn the tunes, put the Meters tape on to hear their count, then turn the volume down and play the piece as slowly as we could. When we turned the tape back up after a few minutes, we were always in front of them. We could never slow down enough. Sometimes our music gets so fast it lends the appearance of slowing down. That's another thing I like about playing arenas. The sound can pile onto itself so deeply that it turns into a big, slow sonic mass.

Page: Trey has tried consciously to feature keyboards more in our arrangements and jams the past few years. I'm still the new guy in the group, after all, and it took me several years to find my space. In 1994 and '95 I began leading jams in ways I hadn't before. In '96 Trey gave me a lot more space by playing his little percussion setup, and the communication between us has kept improving even after he stopped using it. There's a lot more conversational back-and-forth playing between us now, and I have to credit Trey with letting it happen.

BELOW: Providence Civic Center, Providence, Rhode Island, December 29, 1994
BOTTOM: Rosemont Horizon, Chicago, Illinois, October 31, 1995

Trey: Maybe I'm reluctant to change personnel, but I really felt we had something going with Jeff Holdsworth, Mike, Fish, and me. But Mike, in his funny passive-aggressive way, invited Page into the band and started rehearsing songs with him while Fish and I were in Europe together in 1985. Mike neglected to mention the new addition to us even when we called from Europe to rave about the new songs we had. When he did mention Page to us, I believe my timeless reply was, "Phish is a two-guitar band." I was completely wrong. It's hard to be the new guy, but Page, unlike Jeff, was totally into what we were doing. In fact, Page's piano is what sets us apart from the million other two-guitar bands out there. Moreover, no other rock pianist plays with as much incredible understatement as Page, who also has a new synthesizer layering style that has opened up a whole new world of colors and textures we can step into. He truly makes the band something special.

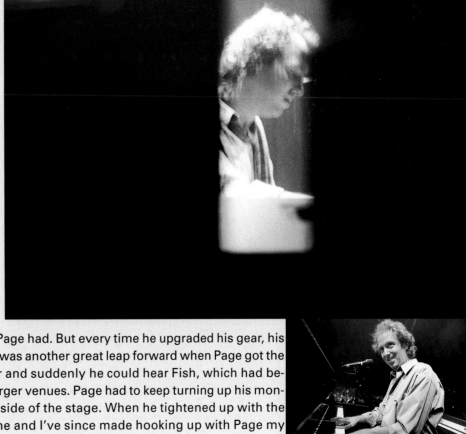

Two things affected Page's entry into the band. First, when he joined I already had a strong musical bond with Fish, and then later with Mike. And second, he had shitty gear. I couldn't deal with the cheesy keyboard sound Page had. But every time he upgraded his gear, his presence in the overall sound also improved. It was another great leap forward when Page got the grand piano. Then he got the Ear Bug monitor and suddenly he could hear Fish, which had become increasingly difficult as we moved into larger venues. Page had to keep turning up his monitors because Fish was way over on the other side of the stage. When he tightened up with the drums, his musical ideas became clearer to me and I've since made hooking up with Page my goal. And I'm always on the lookout for more piano-oriented tunes.

THE MOST STARTLING Phish jams blend four musical equals into something greater than the sum of their parts, and the band's stage setup reflects these democratic aspirations. McConnell's keyboards and Fishman's drum kit bracket the two guitarists. This horizontal alignment not only puts the drummer, usually stuck somewhere in the rear of the stage, on an equal footing with the strings and keyboards, but also allows all four band members to observe one another and exchange extramusical cues and set information on the fly.

Over the years Phish has developed a series of rehearsal exercises that help them break old habits, develop new ways of communicating musically, and level the field so all four instruments may be equally present onstage. The basis for most of these exercises is something the band calls "Including Your Own Hey," which they have used to help get all four members playing in sync. "Including Your Own Hey" begins with one member playing a repeated phrase or pattern. The other three musicians join in with complementary statements, saying "Hey" when they feel comfortably within the groove—with a simultaneous group "Hey" the ideal. Then the musician to the original player's right changes his pattern slightly, the other three refit themselves into this altered statement, and so on in a circular motion.

As Phish dips deeper into the protean groove pool, the band has come to resemble a sly white organometallic hybrid of the funky Meters and Miles Davis, specifically the electric

Miles ensembles that revolutionized jazz-rock fusion between 1968 and 1975. Davis scholar Enrico Merlin has compared those bands to a kaleidoscope, in which a finite number of themes, bass vamps, and personalities were rearranged at every show. Merlin is obsessed with electric Miles in a way certain Phish fans can understand. Studying the two hundred shows Davis played between 1968 and 1975, Merlin identified sixty-nine themes and bass vamps, observing how Davis inserted rhythmic motifs into the middle of songs, as though throwing open a window onto another musical world. Miles had heard the Dead, and vice versa, and was for a time jazz's most fascinating interpreter of the psychedelic imperative.

Davis was also a fan of soul godfather James Brown, who also reached his creative peak during the late sixties. Brown's songwriting method was to bring his "head" arrangements into the studio, which his band would learn, record, then perform onstage with a note-for-note precision Brown believed his audience demanded. Brown hits like "Popcorn," "Sex Machine," and "Papa's Got a Brand New Bag" grooved insistently with geometric precision in emulation of the ritualistic ecstasy of African drummers, until a sudden key change would kick them up a notch. The trick, of course, was knowing when to stick and when to kick.

Page: "Including Your Own Hey" was something we developed and practiced between 1990 and '95, and only rarely thereafter. There were several different varieties of it. Some "Hey" exercises had different members playing counterpoint to other members, while others involved two people dropping out at a time. "Filling the Hey Hole" forced a band member to play only in a spot in the bar where no one else was playing. In other ones we would only vary the volume, timbre, or tempo of what we were playing. All these variations grew out of the original "Including Your Own Hey" exercise.

Fish: Pork Tornado, my other band, is basically a tequila-drinking jam session. We only have one rule: no rehearsals. There have been many sets where we just played one song. We mainly play country covers and some James Brown. Everyone else in the group has played in bar bands their whole lives. When we're onstage, Joe Moore, the singer, just stands there stomping up and down and screaming, "Groove harder! Groove harder! Come on man, hit it!" And you get into it because he's got such a good attitude. After playing three gigs a week for about a month with Pork Tornado, I rehearsed with Phish for a couple of weeks and went back out on the road. About three gigs in, Trey said, "Oh my God! I can't fucking believe how hard you're grooving! Now I can just stand over there and do nothing like I've always wanted." He'd become self-conscious about the whole lead-guitar thing, and now he feels like he can stand there and scratch his balls all night and the show will still go on. It feels easier now.

Page: We're currently going through a funk period. We're also exploring ambient jams that involve me playing synthesizer washes and less piano. Trey and I will create textures over simple drum-and-bass patterns. Mike has been changing his bass lines quite a bit, so we'll jump suddenly from the key we've been jamming in to the fourth above it and hang on that, then switch keys and modulate around. We're also getting back into the sort of spontaneous jamming we used to do at Nectar's, when we'd start with a jam and then go into a song.

Madison Square Garden, October 22, 1996

Trey: We listen to James Brown on the bus because that's what Dominic Placco, our driver, plays. He's got all these James Brown jam tapes.

Fish: My favorite funk drummer is Bernard Purdy of James Brown's band. His syncopation is always simple yet unpredictable. I don't think of myself as a funk drummer but I can work a good middle ground between hard swing and rock. "2001" [as it's come to be known; it's really Richard Strauss's "Also Sprach Zarathustra"] has a nice pop to it. Awhile back we got a James Brown songbook that transcribed all the rhythm parts, and we tried to learn one of those every day.

Our road to funk came from the notion that less is more; funk is sparse. Bob Marley's reggae is very funky in that sense too; everyone does a little bit but it goes a long way. The less we do, the further it goes. If everybody is playing simply, jams tend to get funky. Maybe "funky" is just another word for getting down and communicating. Just like dancing.

Mike: I've been enjoying flipping on my envelope filter and letting the disco groove flow between verses of "2001." We decided to play "2001" after seeing the movie *Being There.* Peter Sellers

plays Chauncey Gardiner, who hasn't left his house in decades. When he finally does, you hear this funky music accompanying him as he walks down the street.

In early 1996 I saw Maceo Parker and the Greyboy All-Stars, who had a big influence on me. We heard a lot of James Brown on the bus during our fall tour that year, and the spacey, funky, acid-jazz grooves Medeski Martin and Wood and some other bands play also got into my head in a big way.

Fish: I was listening to James Brown's *Love Power Peace* album a lot. It's a live show from Paris in 1971.

Some of the guys in Pork Tornado also play with my friend Willis—J. Willis Pratt. When I met Willis, he lived in a Dodge Dart and cooked on a Sterno can. Playing with Willis is a challenge. The guy cannot keep time at all, and erratically adds and subtracts fractions of beats from the beginnings and endings of phrases. His songs have minimal melodies, but they always have incredible hooks. Willis is as left field as Pork Tornado is solid.

Trey: For years I've harped on the notion that a group is greater than the sum of its parts, and almost all the music I like demonstrates that. I don't usually like big solos, but I love King Sunny Ade, Bob Marley's band, the Dead, King Crimson, and James Brown's band. They're the greatest bands ever because they use tiny little bits of harmony and rhythm and make a web, or mesh, out of them. Those bands are bigger than ours, though, so weaving those webs is harder for us, and we've been experimenting with how to do it since 1994 or '95, when we were doing a lot of "Including Your Own Hey" exercises to make us all equally important to the improvisations. The big

OPPOSITE: Tower Records, New York, New York, fall 1996
ABOVE: Providence Civic Center, December 29, 1994

93

frustration of 1996 was that we were still basing everything around "big guitar solos with backup band," or "bass player trying to keep up with frantic drummer" or "keyboard player in background until emerging for big solo." The goal is to have each of us playing with an ear on the other three while feeling completely fulfilled.

Page: It's no mystery to us when we've played a bad set or aren't connecting. It's not like two of us

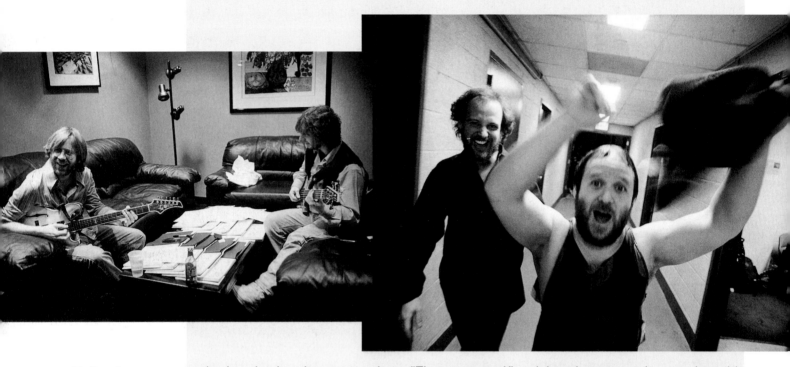

go back to the dressing room and say, "That was great!" and the other two are bummed out. It's more like, "Okay, let's refocus and play a good second set." We don't dwell on the problems because you don't want to get into an analytical head space where you're still analyzing the first set during the second. You want to forget about it. I try to be positive when I'm backstage. All of us always want to play a better second set than the first.

Mike: If we're not having a good gig, we've occasionally yelled at one another backstage, or at least raised our voices. Fish and I probably catch more flack because we're supposed to hold the beat down. If one of us isn't holding it down, everyone suffers. No matter how good a solo is, it doesn't work if there's no support for it underneath.

Fish: We've all gone through periods where we get a little frustrated for one reason or another, but they never last long. Both Trey and I have other musical projects, and Mike is a filmmaker, so we always have time to do our own things. Phish doesn't necessarily have to meet all of our musical needs at once. But in the span of the band's life, all of our musical needs will be addressed sooner or later.

Trey: When we're communicating, the audience hears what we're thinking as though they were inside our heads. But if I can't understand what somebody else in the band is doing, then nobody in the audience can, either. The only reason we're here is because we've all experienced moments when we've transcended our egos and the music has taken on a life of its own. That's what brings people together for a Phish show.

Mike: When we pull off a tough cue or complete a difficult transition, I feel like Maxwell Smart, like a secret agent exchanging clandestine codes with another spy. Sometimes I'll look over to Page

for a cue, get this big smile from him, and think, "What a funny situation. We're in this rock band now, when we could just as easily be working at a chocolate factory." Page used to paint white-chocolate patches on dark-chocolate cows for a living.

Fish: When we criticize one another, it always begins with some qualification like, "I don't mean to tell you what to play, but . . ." When we were learning "Bye Bye Foot," I got Trey to change his guitar solo by saying, "Could you make it not sound so Pink Floydy?" Mike never criticizes another individual. He'll just say something like, "I'm a little starved for melody." He throws out an idea, and we'll all become aware of it.

Mike: At a certain point in my childhood I decided to stop talking as much as I had, because I thought it came off as cooler when people didn't know what you were thinking. That marked the onset of my introversion.

Fish: The benefit of settling down and creating a strong center is that you then have a lot more stretching room. I really feel that musically now. The experiences I've had lately make me feel like

ABOVE LEFT: Memorial Coliseum, Portland, Oregon, October 5, 1995 ABOVE RIGHT: Lowell Memorial Auditorium, Lowell, Massachusetts, May 16, 1995

there's so much more headroom to our playing that we've begun a whole new career, just as if we'd never existed before. I feel like we're finally ready to contribute something original to the tradition of improvised rock music.

Page: The first European tour was so good because we were really relaxed. We wanted to return to that place during the second European tour, but we had great new material to learn, such as "Limb by Limb," "Ghost," "Water in the Sky," "I Saw It Again," "Twist," "Dirt," and "Vultures." They have a certain lightness to them as a group, with overlapping rhythms and repeating lyrics, but without the dark, bitter edge a lot of Tom's songs have. I'll always group those songs together in my mind because they were all presented to me at the same time. They took on a collective personality just from first hearing them in the band room all together.

Fish: When I get too excited, I sometimes try to play sparsely, let a bunch of beats go by, and just float above the whole thing. Sometimes after establishing the groove I start taking things away and let it dissipate. The pulse becomes so strong it's like fly-fishing. You cast the line out and it drifts through the air for a period of time before hitting the water again.

Page: When I lead a jam, nothing in my head is as interesting as simply going for the moment. If the jam isn't raging or heading in a good direction, I'll sometimes fall back on standard riffs and chord progressions. But when it's going well, it can go anywhere. I've also been using a wider assortment of keyboards. The other guys only have guitars and drums to work with, while I have an arsenal of different textures to play with. In general, I find it difficult to switch from one keyboard to another in the middle of a jam. When I'm playing piano, the Fender Rhodes seems a million miles away. But when I listen to a tape and hear another keyboard come in, I always think, "Oh, that's new and exciting."

Fish: We definitely groove more than we used to. I don't listen to us much, but when I hear early tapes I notice that I never just laid down the beat—not even five years ago. It was like pulling teeth to get me to do it, too. Now it's a starting point that makes it easier for me to get outside of the beat eventually, because the rest of the band grooves so well that someone is always holding it down. Trey used to get bummed out because he felt we didn't groove, and he'd become frustrated when he tried to establish grooves himself because his guitar doesn't have enough bottom to give it authority. Mike always wanted to hold down the bottom, but in rock holding down the bottom is supposed to be a team effort between the bass and drums. A jazz drummer, on the other hand, has a lot more leeway to move around with the soloist because the bass player's definitely the bottom.

Trey: What we're doing now is really more about groove than funk. Good funk, real funk, is not played by four white guys from Vermont. If anything, you could call what we're doing cow funk or something. I only know that when I'm playing it, I feel like a big ass floating in the water.

"Chalkdust Torture,"
The Late Show with
David Letterman,
December 30, 1994

Mike Gordon
(FROM LEFT) 1975,
1983, and 1979

Mike: The biggest difference I've noticed lately is that Fish has become surprisingly agile on the kick drum. If I'm playing a bass line, he can mimic it on the kick drum instantly. He concentrated on the cymbals a lot more in the past. We now have a drummer who is simultaneously solid and sensitive. Not only can he lay down heavy grooves, but, like a jazz drummer, he can provide a subtle rhythmic counterpoint to whatever Trey or Page is playing.

Fish: Trey and I used to go on elaborate rhythmic excursions together and play weird interweaving parts, and sometimes we'd lose Page and Mike in the melee.

Trey: Mike is the man these days. His bass playing is his best ever, and he was absolutely the driving force on *Slip Stitch and Pass.* But we had to give him the space to be himself, and all four of us have to be able to be ourselves as well.

Page: One of the great things about Phish is that when a band member brings us something new, we're willing to invest time learning something from it. On our fall 1996 tour Santana percussionist Karl Perazzo spent four days working on Latin grooves with us after he helped us out on *Remain in Light.* We've been trying to learn the Latin tradition more directly, rather than coming at it from the back door, which is how we usually learn new styles.

Mike: Karl jokes around a lot backstage but becomes unflinchingly focused onstage. He taught Trey and Fish some of the building blocks of Latin rhythm. We also asked him to dissect some of our more troubled grooves, like "Funky Bitch" and "Run Like an Antelope," and suggest ways to syncopate the bass and drums.

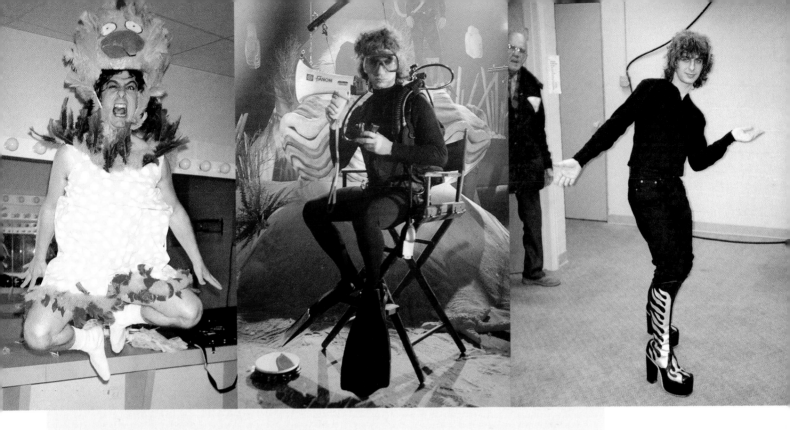

FROM THE SHAVE-AND-A-HAIRCUT Bo Diddley beat of Buddy Holly's "Not Fade Away," to the Beatles' "Do You Want to Know a Secret," to Carlos Santana's raging electric take on the Tito Puente composition "Oye Como Va," Latin beats have long been part and parcel of the rock universe. Salsa, the tango, son, rumba, bossa nova, and so on all combine European harmonies with rhythms brought over on slave ships from Africa. Adding Latin music's tightly meshed rhythms to rock (which itself draws equally strongly from black blues and white folk music) is to open a world of percussive possibilities. With drums and rhythm suddenly at the forefront of rock and pop—in the form of electronica, trance, techno, et cetera—the groove is everywhere you turn, and Phish have discovered new ways to ride it.

Fish: "Punch You in the Eye" was the first Latin beat I learned. It's Latin Rhythm 101 for drum kit. I first figured out that the basic rhythm was a series of pairs of eighth notes lined up, where the second note of one pair would be the first of the next. It's like passing the baton of the rhythm, because they come from rhythm sections where one guy's playing the cowbell pattern, another guy's playing the timbales, and so on. The second beat of the *ba-boom*, the downbeat, becomes the first beat on the cowbell, and the second beat on the cowbell is also the first beat on the snare drum.

Trey: Fish now has several different modes, so he can groove with Mike on these loosely defined time signatures and multiple percussion parts based on Latin music, like "Taste." I was listening to a lot of rootsy Latin music on these Historical Library CDs I bought in Spokane, old scratchy tapes of street music played on different drums. I took a bunch of these rhythms and assembled them on a drum machine for "Limb by Limb," keeping it right on the edge of human possibility to play. Then I gave it to Fish, who learned it to my amazement. And while he strips it down during the song itself,

RIGHT: Burlington, January 19, 1992
OPPOSITE: Trey on drums, Christmas, 1968

playing six against four, you can hear him do the whole thing as a solo at the song's very end.

Page: We played "Taste" at nearly half the shows during the February Europe tour, which is a high percentage for us. "Taste" got into the rotation stronger than anything else off of *Billy Breathes*. Besides having a harder Latin groove than other songs that only hint at different Latin rhythms, "Taste" represented an exciting new style of playing for us because, while it's based on a traditional Latin groove, it's by no means traditional Latin music.

Fish: I've always played drums with the melody rather than the beat going through my head. Theoretically, if any of the other guys lost track of the progression, they should be able to find their place through the drums. It's like the way you can still vaguely hear the tune's melody during a jazz drummer's solo. I don't know if I'm always successful at it, but it's what I go for.

Page: We don't always hear the "one" beat falling in the same place in some extended jams, but we're all experiencing the same pulse even if our "one-two-three-fours" don't line up. We've historically had a tendency to rush as a band. As we've matured, we've acquired a better ability to hang back, play slower songs, and groove. It's difficult to play a slow song, or a ballad, and make it really solid. It takes a lot of concentration and experience. That's why we didn't write many slow songs for a long time; they were all fairly fast and complicated. There are still nights when I wish we'd just slow down or that my playing could be more laid back.

Trey: One of the things that maintains my interest in Phish is that it consists of four equally important personalities. Mitchell Froom, one of my producer heroes, believes democracy in the recording studio can kill an album. He believes you need a dominant personality there. And when we're in the studio, Mike and Fish basically aren't there. But none of our personalities or opinions is more important than the others overall, just like none of us is replaceable, period. Which is why it's so important to us to keep pursuing this one essential thing: the creation of music that represents the unique connection the four of us enjoy.

Fish: The objective is to get beyond the soloing, to get to the point where what you're creating as a whole is better than any solo anyone could play, and it still blows everybody's head off. Playing with Jamie Masefield and the Jazz Mandolin Project gave me another area to stretch out, as well as the opportunity to play with brushes and develop certain aspects of drumming I practice all the time but never really get to use in Phish. I'm comfortable soloing in a swing context although rock drum solos just don't do it for me. If I ever soloed with Phish it would probably make a bunch of people go out for a piss. But the whole reason I'm able to play with Pork Tornado and the JMP and Willis is because I've studied at the Phish School of Music for so long. Phish has always been a band that addressed its weaknesses, and one of the things we have going for us is versatility. At the end of the JMP tour, Chris Dahlgren complimented me on my lis-

tening, and it was very nice to get an objective view of what having been in Phish for fourteen years has done for me as a musician.

Trey: I've played music my entire life. After playing drums in my high school band Space Antelope, picking up the guitar seemed like the most natural thing in the world. It happened so fast that everybody kind of gave me shit about it. But I'd already sung, played piano, and drummed enough so that it was mainly a matter of teaching my fingers to move. I took a couple of classical guitar lessons from a guy in Princeton who was Jose Feliciano's guitar teacher—he reminded me of it constantly. I learned a Bach chorale on a nylon-stringed guitar before getting an electric guitar. I took a few lessons in Burlington from Paul Asbell, but I always discovered that most teachers conveyed just about everything they had to teach in one or two lessons—although you could spend years practicing and learning those things.

Fish: I started playing drums when I was about five, and I've played drums almost my entire life. My parents made me take piano lessons from the lady next door, but I used to say over and over, "I don't want piano lessons, I want drums." Our plumber gave me a drum set for my seventh birthday, and I immediately quit my piano lessons and began emulating John Bonham in the basement. Led Zeppelin is the reason I play music today, and Bonham was the fire under my seven-year-old ass. Zeppelin records are loud and clear, and Bonham's drumming is fairly straight-ahead, so you could hear every part. When it comes to grooves, Zeppelin and Motown records are Drumming 101.

Later on there was always this big monster called jazz in the back of my mind. I couldn't figure out what my favorite jazz drummers were playing, however, so when I was thirteen I took three drum lessons from Dave Hamlin, a good jazz player in Syracuse who taught me how to read music. From then on I could tear jazz apart by ear. I loved learning multiple rhythms that moved my body in abnormal ways that quickly became normal. Drumming at that point became a virtual physical addiction for me. I could probably live without sex a lot easier than I could live without being near a drum set.

OPPOSITE: Boston, December 30, 1996

PHISH INHABIT a unique region triangulated by the improv-rock legacy, experimental music, and the big-ass arena-rock spectacle. When they play as a single instrument, the band are virtuosos of intensity in which open-ended jams become spontaneous compositions. Likewise, songs like "Run Like an Antelope" and "Runaway Jim" inspire feelings of anything-is-possible abandon that coalesce both band and audience into a single energized organism. "Harry Hood," "Antelope," and "Slave to the Traffic Light" traditionally build up to what Chris Kuroda refers to as "the big bang" that once typified the majority of Phish jams. But the current pleasure in these tunes lies in the countless new ways the band finds to achieve sonic climaxes. Band and audience alike approach a Phish show as though it were a festival, with unpredictability the engine constantly transforming the experience into a mystery cruise aboard an intoxicated vessel. As Susannah Goodman's "Bathtub Gin" lyrics state: "We're all in this together and we love to take a bath."

Page: A lot of the songs we decided to put on the back burner didn't even stay away through the Great Went. But what the heck? We made the rules and we can change them. Dropping them was really just an excuse to look at everything we did in a new way.

Trey: Our second Europe tour was unquestionably one of the best we'd ever played until that point.

Page: I started listening to the first Bearsville session when we returned to Europe in the summer of '97. I spent my days off just listening to tapes through headphones, and by the end of the tour I'd come up with a handful of things worthy of playing back to the band. I demoed a few of the cuts I really liked from that twenty hours' worth of jamming to the rest of the band at the very end of the tour as we drove over the Pyrenees mountains on our way to Spain for our last show.

THE CIRCUS COMES TO TOWN: SUMMER TOUR

OPPOSITE: Full
moon over
the Great Went,
Limestone, Maine,
August 16–17, 1997

"I FEEL I'VE NEVER told you the story of the ghost," Anastasio sang in Virginia Beach by way introducing a handful of the new songs the band would concentrate on to their American audience. July 21, 1997, marked the opening night of a summer tour that began with a steamy six-show westward trek across the South before heading up the West Coast. Highlights included guest appearances by drummer Bob Gullotti of the Boston free-jazz ensemble the Fringe and Surrender to the Air. Gullotti joined Phish in Dallas and Austin, adding an improvised layer of percussion to songs he learned on the fly. Phish's newfound affection for big, bulbous grooves could be heard in the Virginia Beach "Ghost," the Phoenix "Gumbo," the Ventura "Bowie>Cities>Bowie," and elsewhere.

The band traveled up the West Coast, playing in some of their favorite haunts along the way. These performances included a long, numinous show at Shoreline Amphitheatre south of San Francisco and two fine nights at the Gorge in George, Washington, an outdoor amphitheater positioned for an awe-inspiring panoramic view of the Columbia River. Anastasio asked Chris Kuroda to cut the lights during the first Gorge show's "Harry Hood" encore. In addition to focusing attention on the music, the gesture also demonstrated how very much Phish's lighting director brings to the party.

"What I mainly try to do is make the color fit the mood," says Chris Kuroda, who first heard Phish at their 1987 Halloween show at Goddard College—"the one where Fish shaved his entire body." He was soon seeing the band at every opportunity, and managed to talk Anastasio into giving him guitar lessons. When the guitarist asked him if knew anyone who would haul gear out to Page's red van after shows for $20, Kuroda volunteered.

"The first show I worked was at the Front in Burlington," Kuroda recalls. "An early taper named Del Martin was helping them in a roadie sort of way, and another guy named Chris Stecher was kind of running their light show, which consisted of eight little lights hung on tripods and a board about the size of a Walkman. The next weekend we played the Stone

Church in New Hampshire. Stecher had to take a leak and asked me to cover for him. 'I don't know how,' I said. 'Nothing to it,' he replied. 'This button turns on the red lights and this one turns on the blue lights. Have fun and I'll be right back.' So he went to the bathroom, and I worked the board during 'Fly Famous Mockingbird,' just flicking between the red and blue lights in time with the song's changes, which I knew from seeing them play so often. After the show I heard Trey go up to Stecher and say, 'Hey, the lights really seemed to click during "Mockingbird." You're starting to get what we're looking for here.' Stecher was like, 'Yeah, thanks a lot.' Later I pulled Trey aside and said, 'I was running the lights during "Mockingbird." The day before the next gig, Trey called me up and said, 'Chris won't be able to make our next show, and we want you to run our lights.' I said, 'I don't know anything about lights.' Trey replied, 'We'll figure it out together.'" That was March 30, 1989, and Kuroda has been running lights for the band ever since.

Kuroda's lights synergize with the band like a fifth instrument that instantaneously interprets, heightens, and shapes what is already music of considerable drama and color. Perched behind Languedoc and his sound board, Kuroda operates a large and complex virtual kaleidoscope. His lights are a constantly changing ballet of looks, cues, and positions. "All I do, all night long, is count," he claims. "I have to be just ahead of the band because of the half-second lag between hitting a button and the lights' reaction. So I watch for the lights to flash on the upstroke of the button I'm hitting. It took practice to get it down, but now I can do it in my sleep. It's all in the upstroke."

Onstage, the band communicates largely through quick glances, and Kuroda is obliged to watch and listen to them as intently as they listen to one another. "It used to be mandatory for me to attend band practice eight hours per day for weeks at a time, listening and learning. I'd set up lights in the practice room and jam with them." Kuroda currently operates three separate and incompatible systems (Vari-Lites, Altstars, and Cyberlights), aided by two assistants with whom Kuroda communicates over headsets. With approximately twelve hundred programmed cues and color changes at his disposal, "I need to give the right numbers to the right guy at the right moment on top of counting the whole time while trying to pick up every little nuance of what's going on onstage. It's a lot of listening, a lot of counting, and a lot of talking, all at the same time and pretty much nonstop."

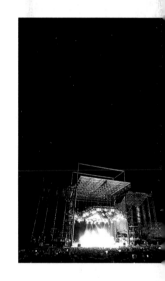

The lights stayed on as Phish headed home across the Midwest. In Darien Lake, New York, the band were joined onstage by Ken Kesey and the Merry Pranksters for a set that demonstrated that East Coast avant-garde arena rockers and West Coast theatrical dadaists mix somewhat less easily than you might expect. But all categories were cast aside two days later, when the Great Went went down in Limestone, Maine.

When I spoke to the band in Phoenix, where the band and crew had enjoyed a searing day off by floating down a river on inner tubes, the talk turned to the band's audience, its expectations, and the price of success.

Trey: The Phoenix "Gumbo" was another jam I want to put on an album someday. We played with so much space, it was a revelation. Part of it was still about learning how to play in a big room, where spacious playing works better than making a lot of noise.

Page: I looked forward to taking what we learned playing in European clubs—new ways of jamming, new attitudes, and fresh perspectives—and then adding twenty thousand people to the mix.

Mike: We tour for a lot of the same reasons as the people who follow us around. We're out to have fun, not just to accumulate fans or make money. We're out there for adventure, and in that sense we're all showing up at the gig for the same reason.

Page: Much of Phish's appeal stems from the excitement we've all felt when we suddenly discovered a band we'd never heard of that also happened to have a huge back catalog of music. Maybe it's even still around, only you don't hear it on the radio or see it on MTV. That's how I discovered the Dead and the Velvet Underground, who opened up new musical worlds for me. Likewise, Phish isn't a household word—or even a word at all—in large parts of the country. We simply don't exist. Discovering us through word of mouth gives listeners a sense of personal attachment to us that wouldn't exist if we were force-fed to audiences or served up as flavor of the week. And we can be appreciated on several different levels—through our lyrics, touring history, set lists, the Gamehendge mythology, or just in the moment. We'll continue to find places to play where they've never heard of us. So, see you next year in Bangkok.

WHEN THE CIRCUS comes to town in the form of Phish and their thousands of nomadic followers, it takes a concerted effort of the band's management and crew, the venue's staff and security, and the ticket holders to make the whole enterprise come off with a minimum of hitches. After playing well over one thousand shows during the past fourteen years, band and management have both refined, and subtly redefined, the way a rock act tours. Phish's history of drawing guaranteed capacity crowds makes promoters and venues receptive to the band's needs, and while Phish have never gone so far as to demand the removal of brown M&M's from their dressing room, a detailed set of security requirements and a comprehensive contractual "rider" stipulating the band and crew's needs structure the details of their appearances in order to provide the best music in the best physical circumstances.

"The thing about our show," says tour manager Richard Glasgow, "is that once you get the kids in the building and clear the perimeter, it's the most boring show in the world as far as security is concerned. They're neither violent nor malicious, they don't crowd surf or mosh. They just love to dance."

"You've got to watch the spinners," warns security director John Langenstein, "and make sure they don't fall down the stairs. The inexperienced new kids who come to spin, especially if they've been drinking, will sometimes get dizzy and—*boom!*—bite the dust. You can definitely tell the experienced spinners from the novices. The experienced spinners won't even stop between songs. They find a beat somewhere in their head and just keep on twirling."

"My favorite thing about the crowd is the way it resembles a family," says Bart Butler, who supervises security inside the venue. "If a security guy picks on one of them, dozens of other audience members will get in his face throughout the night. And they hate scalpers. One kid will grab a handful of scalper tickets, run into a crowd, and throw them into the air."

ABOVE: Outside the Corestates Spectrum, Philadelphia, Pennsylvania, December 28, 1996 OPPOSITE: The taping section, Fleet Center, December 31, 1996

As devotees of the unexpected rock experience have known for decades, going on tour is among the few real adventures left for the young. Scraping up money for gas, bad food, and tickets, and hitting the road with Phish is still in the realm of possibility for the several thousand wookies, gobis, prep-school hippies, frat lads, spinners, lawyers, waiters, and code writers who follow the band from show to show for days or weeks at a time, living in a peculiar, temporary world separate but equal to consensus reality. And thanks to these freeway flyers, the Phish musical experience transcends a show-to-show rhythm, expanding to encompass multinight runs, geographical tour segments, and, by extension, the entire tour itself.

Like sports fans, Phish cognoscenti maintain an ongoing buzz of high expectations. This segment of the audience accords Phish the most authentic coin of the realm simply by *paying attention* to the band night after night in city after city. Some fans mythologize the musicians, finding glory, solace, or disaster in a guitar riff or bass line. Others enter the fold through poring over stats, timing jams, and analyzing set lists with Epicurean finesse. Since seating for tapers is made available at virtually every show, Phish completism is available to anyone with the modem, blanks, and postage to pursue it.

At the end of the night, however, each fan has her or his own version of what Phish is. Because a rock band's persona is ultimately completed by the fans who buy its records and T-shirts, attend its shows, trade tapes, and pass along the good word to others in late-night dorm-room revelations. Like the two onstage chess games the band played against the audience during its fall 1995 tour—exchanging moves before and after sets—the band/audience give-and-take is an ongoing group-mind game involving teases, expectations, and a win-win delivery of the musical goods.

Fish: Sometimes I ask myself, "God, do I really want to be part of something that involves a crowd of people following me around?" The other side of it is that I've been meeting community-oriented younger musicians striving for a group interaction greater than themselves. I've met a lot of kids who follow us because of the Grateful Dead thing, which seemed to get out of control toward the end, as though the pests had destroyed the cornfield. I suppose on some level the parasites are unavoidable; but if our music provides something people don't get elsewhere, if it's hitting some kind of communal nerve that makes people want to live a life that parallels what we do musically, then great.

Mike: Woody Allen, Terry Gilliam, and David Lynch are my favorite contemporary filmmakers. In

-♡♡-
Jane

school I was really into French New Wave directors like Jean-Luc Godard and Francois Truffaut. As a kid, I really liked James Bond films because I wanted to *be* James Bond. On the road I often feel as though I'm going from town to town on a secret mission while the locals work their nine-to-five jobs. And the idea that all those great musicians would leave their little jobs to play with a band made *The Blues Brothers* a life-changing experience for me.

Fish: Celebrity is the only aspect of my job that sucks. It's definitely a bummer when people come to your house late at night and piss on your mailbox. One time a guy walked right through the front door of my house at four-thirty in the morning with a beer in his hand wanting to shake hands. In all fairness, though, he did call the next day to apologize.

Mike: I'm always imitating everything, and one day I started imitating the people who come up to us before, during, and after the show to say things like, "You gawz were so hot tonight!" This led to a complete lexicography of this particular type of fan, known in its noun form as the "gawzer." There's also a verb form—"Page is getting thoroughly gawzed out there." I guess anyone who achieves public-eye status has to deal with fans, and we're lucky our fans are basically nice, down-

to-earth people. But there's a certain fan/musician dialogue you almost can't avoid. You want to meet someone you really respect, but you don't have anything to say to them. So you end up making these assumptions about one another. The musician assumes he or she is having a conversation with a normal person, forgetting that the other person is experiencing a rare opportunity for interaction with this idealized figure. And the person having the rare opportunity doesn't bear in mind how commonplace an activity this is for the musician.

Trey: If you wanted to start a band in the early eighties, the Dead provided a complete revelation about how to play good music. If you take from them what you should, however, you won't sound anything like them, which is the weird thing about Dead cover bands. The cool thing about the Dead was that each member was able to express himself as an individual within the framework of the Dead as a group. So Phil Lesh played the bass like Phil Lesh, and it worked in the Dead mesh, and Bob Weir played like Bob Weir. But put any of them in their other bands, like Bobby and the Midnights, and it didn't work as well because it was just some people backing up a famous guy. In the context of the Dead, however, they collectively created a totally unique and amorphous kind of music that perfectly reflected that particular collection of personalities.

AFTER YEARS of Phish hedging about their overly presumed affinity to the Dead, it was interesting to hear Anastasio make the spiritual affinity between the two bands explicit, as he did at Shoreline at the end of the second set during "Weekapaug Groove." Phish had covered several Dead tunes during their first couple of years together but soon dropped them to avoid the onus of being pigeonholed as yet another Dead cover band. Aside from the fact that Phish, like the Dead, prefer to allow interesting jams to occur naturally rather than forcing them, you'd be hard-pressed to find many Phish songs resembling Hunter/Garcia or Weir/Barlow compositions. Enmeshed in the working-class politics and emotions of another era entirely, the Dead were thoroughly products of the West Coast's beat/hippie scene; Phish, on the other hand, came of age on the East Coast during the postpunk eighties.

Mike: When I was a freshman at the University of Vermont in 1983, I traveled to Dead shows when I should have been studying electrical engineering. A guy in my dorm used to razz me by saying, "Getting together and playing like the Dead is the easiest thing in the world. You just go up and down mixolydian scales together." There's an element of truth to that, of course, but you also need years of experience (or moments of true abandon) to know *when* to go up the scale and when to come down.

Trey: We played a couple of Dead songs when Phish first got together in 1983, and I said, "That's it. I'm not listening to the Dead anymore or going to any Dead shows." They were too imposing an influence and I was afraid of becoming the next baby Dead band to come down the pike. So I completely ended my relationship with their music for about seven years.

Garcia's not the only guitarist I avoided. Once Bruce Hampton asked me, "Did you listen to a lot of Pat Metheny?" and that was it. Rickie Lee Jones dissed Joni Mitchell once, which Mitchell chalked up to what she called the Kill Mommy Syndrome. I listened to Jimmy Page—first big rock influence—fanatically in eighth grade, and then Jimi Hendrix, who represented the next level of rock guitar. I saw Pat Metheny's original group during tenth grade and became obsessed. He was ripping it up with his single-line storytelling style back then, and I probably saw him ten times over the next year. I was still into Led Zeppelin and heavy metal when I transferred to Taft. My next-door neighbor there, Chris, was really into the Dead, but I just didn't buy it. He took me to a show, and I didn't even pay attention. It was too boring for me. Then he took me again, I took a couple hits of blotter, and I got it. Yes, it's a cliché, but isn't that always what happens?

Mike: Garcia used to compare the Grateful Dead to licorice: You either love it or hate it. It can be challenging to explain to non–Dead-lovers what made them special without diminishing the expe-

rience, but I like trying. The Dead's main appeal for me was the way they combined my favorite things in music: the down-home, the funky, and the improvisational. They took traditional American music—bluegrass, country, and blues—and mixed in a funky sort of rock and roll, and then threw all the cards in the air by jamming. You don't get that mix very often, and especially not played by serious musicians who dedicated themselves to it for decades. They never gave up on improvisation or let it become merely a token part of the mix. And the Dead played in an almost African manner. Each musician contributed to a groove with clear, distinct parts that formed a whole without any single instrument dominating the mix.

Trey: When I listened to the Dead much later, after having learned a lot more about harmony and come a long way as a musician myself, I heard things in it I'd never realized were going on. The level Jerry Garcia was playing at was simply astonishing. A lot of Dead jams are modal excursions from a single tonal center, and Garcia was playing harmonically outside in the same way that John Coltrane was. After spending a lot of time studying the different scales that take you out to the five chord of any tonal center, I realized Garcia had been doing that all along.

Mike: I don't listen to the Dead very much these days, but I watched a couple of their videos recently. What got to me was the light and bouncy lilting quality of their jams. Lilt and bounce are harder to achieve than you might expect. The very same music can be a complete chore to plow through one night yet be impossible *not* to groove to the next time I play it. It's amazing how a song like "Fee" every once in a while achieves a level of bounciness so far above all the other times we've played it. We'll all say, "This was definitely the best 'Fee' we've played in years," and I'll think it was due to the level of bounciness we achieved, a certain playfulness where every note matters deeply yet feels utterly carefree at the same time. If each note mattered in a heavy kind of way, the whole thing would sound bogged down; and if each note didn't matter at all, it sounds as though you simply don't care, empty and passionless. But what gives the Dead and our music its lilting quality, when it's there, are notes that sound as heavy as a boulder and light as a feather at once.

Trey: I was obsessed with Garcia's playing through my freshman year in college. I couldn't get over his sense of melody and direction. He was the opposite of, say, Eric Clapton, who, as a B. B. King fan, was much more interested in the intensity of a single note. Jerry could take an eight-measure phrase and give it logical musical sense over a long period of time. The longer I listened to him, the more I became interested in his influences, primarily bluegrass and Django Reinhardt, who I still listen to a lot. Django played standards like "Night and Day" and "Honeysuckle Rose," concise three-minute jazz-guitar versions of some of the greatest melodies ever created. Garcia took Django's melodic improvisation into the next dimension. You always heard the melody when he soloed, and it was as beautiful and heart wrenching as it was spacey and psychedelic—everything you could want, in a single package.

Mike: Phil Lesh's bass lines sometimes sound clunky or even hokey to me, but I still have to resist being influenced by his unbelievable melodic bounce. His playing isn't as pattern-based as most bass players'; it varies from measure to measure. And while it might seem like haphazard scale

running to some, it actually results from a chemistry that evolved over decades of experience playing with the same group of musicians.

Trey: It had to have been a heavy burden being Garcia, but it doesn't necessarily have to be that way. Frank Zappa, for example, had no problem at all being Frank. He loved being Frank, and there's something simple and inspiring about that. But when the Dead were playing really well, I couldn't tell who was playing what much of the time. My ear wanders constantly from musician to musician as though the band were a single instrument. At the same time, Garcia was also one of the great American singers. I mean, when I listen to the Dick's Picks CDs, I always skip ahead to "Stella Blue" because listening to the guy sing is as exquisitely heart wrenching as hearing him play guitar.

I listen to Del McCoury, who used to be in Bill Monroe's band, and he reminds me that Garcia was as important a traditional American songwriter and singer as Monroe. He was so damn good he may have been cursed by his own talent. If the band wasn't playing well and Garcia took a solo, it was enough. You could spend the whole night just listening to Jerry sing and play. But when the band was on, he became part of a band at its highest level of magical greatness. Since no one in Phish has that kind of individual talent, the essence of what we try to do lies in developing our group sound.

Mike: Phish and the Dead share certain musical values. We don't make music to revolt against societal institutions in an overtly political way. But at the same time we both try to break radical new ground in whatever small ways we can. Not that our respective bands always reflect sweetness and light. Both the Dead and Phish explore some pretty dark and scary places as a way to celebrate life in all its diversity.

The big differences between us and the Dead are A, the sixties are history, and B, they typified a West Coast mentality utterly foreign to us. They were also more deeply rooted in the American folk music tradition than we are, while we're probably a little more experimental than they were.

Trey: I was obsessed with Jimmy Page, Jeff Beck, Pat Metheny, and Robert Fripp in high school, and Hendrix, Zappa, and Garcia afterward. But if you don't want to sound like a second-rate version of your idols, you definitely have to go through your "kill-Mommy" phase.

Mike: Yes, both the Dead and Phish attract a similar obsessed demographic. Even Bob Weir says the one thing he always disliked about Deadheads was how they only listen to the Grateful Dead.

Fish: Ten years ago, the last thing I wanted was a home base. I loved living completely on the hoof and found the idea of home limiting. Now I'm experiencing the opposite. Living my life that way was actually becoming more of an energy sink than an energy source. When I go on tour now, after recharging my battery at home, I have a lot more juice than I used to.

Mike: Trey is the most domestically entrenched of us all—but he's also the wildest band member.

Trey: My Italian grandmother, Granmoony, was my greatest pal and confidante when I was growing up. For a long time I questioned whether it was possible for a traveling musician to still have a solid family life. Then we did a tour opening for Carlos Santana, a righteous guy in the best sense of the word. He has three kids and talked about his family all the time. "Never develop your per-

OPPOSITE: The Gorge, August 2, 1997
LEFT: Trey sits in with Carlos Santana, Finger Lakes Performing Arts Center, Canandaigua, New York, July 28, 1992.

sonal image on the road," he told me. "When you're surrounded by people telling you how great you are, it's all bullshit. Go home for a week, empty the garbage, mop the floor, change a lot of diapers, and then consider your place in life. And give something back to the community." The next time we toured with him, I felt bad because our bands were in weird moods and weren't connecting as well as they had. When I mentioned this to Carlos, he told me not to worry about it. "If you have a long career," he said, "you're going to have ups and downs. Look at me. I've played stadiums, I went back to playing theaters, and now I'm on my way back up again. You'll see. Next tour I could be opening for you." We were like, "Sure, get out of here." But Carlos knows what's going on. He's been playing music for a long time.

Page: As an artist, it doesn't help me to read bad things about myself, so I don't. It's not that I don't enjoy having my ego stroked by positive reviews, because I do; I'm human, and everybody likes being complimented. But if I'm not going to pay attention to the negative things, then I shouldn't pay attention to the positive things, either.

Fish: I truly in my heart could give a flying fuck what anyone thinks about what we do. About a year ago I realized that, short of cutting off my arms and legs, nothing would ever hinder my desire to play drums or diminish the joy I get from playing them.

Trey: I really admire musicians like Miles Davis and Bob Dylan, because they completely ignored the critics and naysayers and forged ahead with the music they truly believed in. When Dylan played electric at the '65 Newport Folk Festival, he practically caused a riot. Then he took off on a yearlong tour where he was booed offstage nightly, but he just kept going. His strength of conviction is what makes him a great artist. I think that the one quality that is shared by all great artists is individuality. To me, the greatest goal as a musician is to sound like yourself. Since everyone's life experience is different, sounding like yourself would be to sound totally original and different. I'm not there yet, but I'm trying.

Mike: The last shot of the Clifford Ball video that ran on MTV was the best thing about it. It's a

OPPOSITE: Fleet Center, December 31, 1996
ABOVE: Pregame sound check of the national anthem, the Great Western Forum, Inglewood, California, December 3, 1996

slow-motion shot taken by a guy running through the crowd with a Steadicam on his shoulder. You see frat boys staring right into the camera as Trey sings "the crowd intrudes all day." This moment pretty well represents how the band feel about meeting people sometimes when communication is tainted by assumptions. It's quite a touching moment. The crowd doesn't usually intrude on me, however. I'm the guy who usually bikes or golf-carts out into the parking lot before the show. I still relate to either side of the fan/musician relationship.

Trey: When someone asked how he felt about fame, Albert Einstein replied, "It sure gets in the way of your work." It's true, and sometimes I think, "Jesus Christ! I've spent countless hours the past two years dealing with my career, conferring with managers, and giving interviews when I should have been practicing guitar and writing songs." But for the most part, fame is great. I get to sing the national anthem at Lakers games, and people do my laundry for me on tour.

Page: Beyond the other three guys' opinions being important to me, I don't get worked up about how people perceive us. Why should a fan's opinion count for more than a critic's, or our manager's? I'd rather hear what someone seeing us for the first time has to say about the experience. Sometimes we respond directly to our audience. When we started playing "Theme from the Bottom" live, we took out the riff that preceded the guitar solo on the album version. But a guy wrote Trey to say he liked how that section kicked off the jam, and he was right. So we put it back in.

Trey: There was a lot of hoopla surrounding us between about 1994 and '97, but we soldiered past it. Now we're just a band again. We felt like people didn't know about us for a decade, then they learned about us, and now they don't give a shit anymore because they're on to something else. The media hype is over, and we're safe again.

Fish: It might have taken a couple of years longer, or maybe not, but I don't think it would have hindered our career at all if we'd never done a single interview. The whole Phish thing was growing by word of mouth anyway. My musical idols are the Residents, a theatrical San Francisco band that wears eyeballs on their heads so nobody knows who they really are. That's my ideal. They got it right. They built a following of loyal fans based solely on the quality of their work—but no one knows their faces. They only experience the upside of whatever fame they have.

Trey: I got into this because making music in the basement with my friends became an addiction. I *need* to play music, it's my ultimate release. You can't imagine the feelings I have onstage. It's a very self-centered experience in a certain way, but it's like a dream to me. When I walk offstage, my feet feel six inches off the ground. Then somebody says something like, "The bus is leaving in fifteen minutes," and I'm back to earth again and can't wait until the next night.

Mike: We played UVM's Earth Day two or three times. People don't realize how long it took us not only to break into venues across the country, but to break into our own college. It even took awhile to get a gig at Slade Hall, the hippie dorm. It was run by a committee that went over tapes with a fine-tooth comb. Some of the members were cool, others just hated us. The venue's in a tiny basement where they cook their own food, so it has a peculiar aroma. We played some of our best early gigs there but were never totally accepted.

Fish: At one point in our career everything was entirely positive. Everybody who heard Phish liked us, and nobody else cared. Now we've reached the point where it's cool to hate us, which is okay with me. It tests our mettle.

Page: I don't feel overwhelmed by success. I love it. But I'm not as front and center as Trey is, and don't attract as many fans. A thousand barefoot children aren't dancing on *my* lawn.

Fish: We always had the luxury of letting things grow slowly. Our families supported us in college, and none of us has been destitute. Not that we were slackers, either. I've worked as a dishwasher and cab driver, and made maternity bathing suits for a while. I also moved toilets out of one warehouse and television cable into another.

Page: Our summer tour included great shows at the Gorge and Shoreline, finishing up the Great Went. The Went was a bit more focused and down-to-business than the Clifford Ball, which had all the magic of any first-time, I-can't-believe-this-is-happening event.

IN AUGUST 1996 Phish threw a party and everybody came. The Clifford Ball attracted sixty thousand contented campers to a decommissioned air force base in Plattsburgh, New York, where the band played six sets and a rolling three-in-the-morning flatbed-truck jam amid an aeronautics-themed environment, the construction of which was executed in large part by Vermont builder Russ Bennett.

By this point in their career, Phish had already played more than a thousand live shows together. With that accumulated experience under their belts, they were eager to take everything they'd learned about putting on a show and apply it to a single event that took the audience into consideration in every respect. The Clifford Ball, as well as the following summer's Great Went, also afforded Phish the opportunity to test the limits of the "wouldn't-it-be-cool-if?" credo they'd adhered to from the band's outset. When it came to the Ball and the Went, the sky was the only limit, not that they didn't manage to integrate that into both events as well. The Clifford Ball's aviation theme was inspired by eponymous air-mail pioneer Clifford Ball, heralded as "a beacon of light in the world of flight."

Named after a minor character from the David Lynch film *Twin Peaks: Fire Walk with Me*, the journey-themed Great Went took place August 16 and 17, 1997, on the decommissioned Loring Air Force Base in the northern Maine hamlet of Limestone (five hours north of Portland by car), and drew sixty-five thousand fans from every state in the country. Spread over eight hundred acres, the Great Went's environment was conceived mainly by Burlington artist Lars Fisk and built by a team of Vermonters led by Russ Bennett. A thousand employees worked on the Went, which was designed to be more loosely environmental, more "vibe"-oriented, and, especially, more *musical* than the Clifford Ball. As cars rolled off the highway, ticket holders were greeted by a fifty-foot-high "thumbs-up" mural painted on a building. The spirit of excursion was also symbolized by a car—eventually auctioned off—spinning on a rotating hydraulic jack.

Taking inspiration from nineteenth-century formal Italian gardens, Fisk and Bennett conceived and created a cornfield maze and fabric topiary sculpted into illuminated tree cones that they arranged to form pathways. Elsewhere, a field of oversized, neon-orange glove-shaped wind socks signified that we were once again on a decommissioned air base, one noted for several 1969 UFO sightings. Oddest of all was the ten-foot-high plastic-daisy shower curtain that encircled the Port-O-Let Piazza's relief facilities and elevated bathtub/fountain centerpiece. Strung between telephone poles, clotheslines hung with oversized articles of clothing framed the stage and gave the grounds a backyard feel. The audience basked in the vastness of the sky amid the trappings of a psychedelic suburbia. The scene recalled the picnic spirit of the relatively intimate and fondly remembered outdoor Phish shows held during the late eighties and early nineties at Arrowhead Ranch, Townshend Park, Ian McClain's pig roasts, and on Amy Skelton's horse farm.

BELOW AND OVERLEAF: The flatbed-truck jam, the Clifford Ball, August 17, 1996

Surrounded by the 1.3-mile-long "Great Wall of Limestone," the concert site's architectural centerpiece was a surreal town square in which people could get small, watch themselves watching artisans, and eat reasonably priced fresh local chop. Among the miniature structures were a post office, an observatory, a Swiss-cheese house, a bubble house filled with soapsuds spewing from wall-mounted bubble machines, and a "Housewife Cockfight" house in which duels between bizarre household appliances were fought. Music filled both the air and the airwaves. Pirate-sized, free-form Radio WENT broadcasted throughout the weekend, simulcasting all

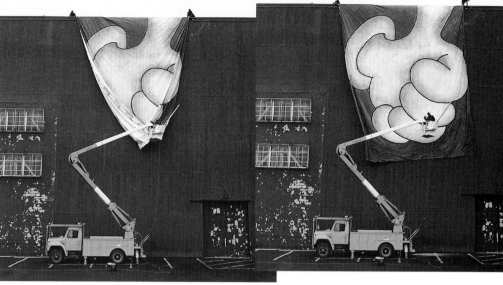

Phish's performances in stereo along with audio verité samplings of the crowd, and band archivist Kevin Shapiro's vault gems. The first evening's fireworks (monitored by the world's largest fire truck) were larger than most towns' Fourth of July celebrations.

Like the Clifford Ball and the band's New Year's Eve shows, the Great Went had the feel of a summation—of both the summer tour and the band's career to date. But where the Clifford Ball had seemed like a momentous occasion the band strived to live up to, the Great Went provided a setting in which Phish sounded like a band completely at home with itself and its audience. And home, they say, is where the art is. Performing three sets each day, with a late-night synthesizer jam in between, the band gave itself plenty of time to stretch out both onstage and off. Band and audience baked and reveled in an atmosphere of blissed-out energy release and pure fun. An old-fashioned happening in nineties garb, the Went, like Phish's music, gave back to the audience what they put into it, and then some.

Some attendees went above and beyond the call of duty. More than eleven hundred campers volunteered to pose for nude Sunday-morning photos taken by New York–based photographer Spencer Tunick as part of his series of public group nudes. Hundreds of others, unfortunately, had to be turned away when all the releases had been spoken for. The resulting image was submitted to *The Guinness Book of World Records* as the world's largest nude photo but was rejected as being unfit for a family publication.

The Went began at precisely four-twenty on Saturday afternoon with the loping one-drop reggae beat of "Makisupa Policeman," its lyrics (by third-grader Tommy Marshall) declaring, "Hey Makisupa policeman, policeman came to my house." And a year after the Clifford Ball, we were once again *chez* Phish, a pleasure compound in which a band-picked "Safety" force replaced the traditional rock security contingent (Hell's Angels they were not). Phish then completed the aborted "Harpua" with which they had ended the Clifford Ball. It felt like a benediction, and they were off.

Mike: When we first discussed the Clifford Ball, we sat down and tried to figure out what worked and didn't work with big concerts—dealing with bad parking situations and that sort of thing. Two things we immediately eliminated were virtual-reality booths and mimes. And virtual mimes.

Trey: I loved the flatbed-truck jam at the Clifford Ball and would love to release it on an album someday. It was an utterly eerie experience to glide past campfires in a musical trance at four in the morning, just rolling along and watching the landscape go by. We really just put these things together to get our jollies, and we've been doing that for a long time. But if the hot dog was a big toy for us to play with, the Clifford Ball and Great Went were more on the scale of creating our own entire theme parks.

Mike: I thought I'd be most interested in the filming being done during the Great Went, but I ended up getting off on things I didn't even know would happen, like the Housewife Cockfight with the little vacuum cleaners, the foaming booth, the car rotating in the middle of the field, and even the post office. Our artist friend Jim Pollock's booth was cool because it was built entirely without ninety-degree angles. I just took it all in. It was not unlike attending a concert as a fan, except that I had a golf cart.

Trey: I remember most of the Great Went— even the synthesizer jam. I can't wait to get back there for another weekend of throwing away all my worries and indulging myself in Phish fantasyland. It's self-indulgent in the best sort of way: We're the only band around, and we play as long as we want to. We've always been stage pigs, mainly because it's such an escape for us. It really comes down to that: The Went and its ilk are just oversized extensions of that, or a childhood fantasy come true. How often do you get to drive around in a golf cart with your name on it? I didn't want it to end. In fact, I wanted to add a third day in 1998, but everybody thought it would be too much for the staff.

Fish: Rock is traditionally about pissing off your parents, and sometimes we're accused of being too likable. But the risks and adventures we take are musical rather than sociological. A good band doesn't necessarily have to rub everyone the wrong way. The Herbie Hancock Quartet politely blew my head open at the '97 New Orleans Jazz Festival, and only a total moron would think they weren't taking risks.

Trey: The main lesson I took home from the Went is the importance of delegation. I got tired of being the guy who has to answer all the last-minute questions. Fish can be in charge of the nude picture this year. He'd be great at it. Those photos convinced me the human race is bound for extinction. All those little pink sacs laid out on the runway like that looked much too fragile to survive.

HAVING INVITED everybody to an after-hours disco party, the band popped up late Saturday night on a portable stage set up on the fringes of the campground. There, behind four separate sampler/synthesizer racks, the band offered a spontaneous update of a 1970s Kraftwerk set. Rather than blasting the techno grooves everyone expected, however, the band instead delivered forty-five minutes of eerie, discombobulated electronic ravings.

Trey: Our friend Myndy K. arranged for a group of contortionists and dancers to come onstage during one of our Madison Square Garden shows [10/22/96]. Afterward, she took me downtown with some of her drag-queen friends to a club called Jackie 60 where we heard an amazing DJ. The grooves were incredible, and I felt a distinct similarity between the club vibe and our shows: everybody getting down in search of that transcendent groove. So when we were in Amsterdam a few months later, I wandered into a dark little store and bought a stack of incredible techno CDs you could use to create your own rave. The Great Went concept was to spin discs and play synthesizers over them, but it didn't work technically, because there were four of us rather than a single DJ. So we collected a bunch of keyboards instead for a couple of late-night-hours' worth of synthetic cacophony.

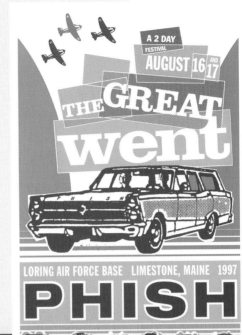

OPPOSITE: **The Great Went: Gates open at** 1:00 P.M. **on Saturday.**
THIS PAGE AND OVERLEAF: **The nude photo, Sunday morning,** 10:00 A.M.

THE FOLLOWING AFTERNOON, the Bangor Symphony Orchestra performed two of Anastasio's favorite compositions, Debussy's "String Quartet No. 2" and Stravinsky's "L'Histoire du Soldat." Then a glider pilot equipped with ear monitors improvised an exquisitely graceful aerial ballet inspired by the orchestra's rendition of Debussy's "Claire de Lune," touching down on an adjacent runway in perfect synchronicity with both the work's conclusion as well as the full moon's appearance just above the horizon.

Band and audience shared an undeniable simultaneous peak experience during Sunday's second set, when a raucous "Down with Disease" resolved into the we're-in-this-together intoxication of "Bathtub Gin." The deceptively straight-ahead "Gin" jam achieved liftoff via a relentlessly ascending hyperdriven riff that simultaneously evoked Big Jay McNeely's honking saxophone, Aretha Franklin's gospel soul, and Sly Dunbar and Robbie Shakespeare's hard-rock reggae. Having brought the song to a peak and held it there for as long as possible, Phish set the time machine on reverse. Their rendition of Bill Monroe's "Uncle Pen" provided a breather as well as a launching pad for the most spaced-out version of the "2001" theme to date, one that hatched open a beguiling series of minor interior jams before ascending to its C-major resolution.

Anastasio brought the music to a halt to take note of the unique relationship Phish shares with its audience. He observed that, in the spirit of that hitherto unspoken "mutual energy," the band would now add its material creation to those of the Went attendees who had been contributing to a steadily ascending wooden Watts Tower of a structure being constructed near the stage. During the set, two band members at a time had dropped out of the music as the spirit moved them in order to paint on oddly shaped wooden canvases. As Phish played a soft "art jam" dominated by McConnell's churchy organ chords played over the "2001" progression, the four band creations were assembled into a single spotlit piece that was given to the audience, who slowly passed it overhead by hand the several hundred feet from the stage to the tower.

A beautiful "Harry Hood" followed, but Anastasio interrupted its tension-revving jam to request that Kuroda cut the lights as he had done two weeks earlier at the Gorge. This time, however, the darkened runway switched on spontaneously with hundreds of arcing glow sticks of varying incandescent colors that lit up

the night like a gigantic artificial-life computer program—the first of the intermittent "glow-stick wars" that would pop up at subsequent shows. Finally, immediately following a cover of Los Lobos's "When the Circus Comes to Town" and its warning about "the day I burn this old place down," a thirty-foot cantilevered match tipped and ignited the now-completed tower sculpture, which burst into flames as "Tweezer Reprise" brought down the curtain on another memorable all-Phish weekend.

Trey: The second set of the second day of the Went was unbelievable. I almost lost it when the glow sticks began to fly under the full moon hanging right above the sculpture during "Harry Hood."

Mike: Fish, Page, and I used to live with our friend Brian Long in a red house across the street from the Burlington Harry Hood bottling company. Fish used to make these soups by throwing all the food in the house—lettuce, cumin, raisins, everything—into one big brown pot. You'd have to eat it because nothing else was left, it was all in the soup, and we'd live on it for weeks at a time. We kept getting junk mail addressed to our house's previous tenant, Mr. A. Minor. One piece was a form letter with his name embedded in all the sentences, saying, "Thank you Mr. Minor."

Trey: In the summer of 1985 Fish and I went to Europe with our friend Pete Cottone. We flew there to travel around and play music on the street, which sometimes worked and sometimes didn't. We eventually ran out of money and really had to scrape by. I played my mini electric guitar, Fish played Flexitone drums, and Pete played bongos. Some of the music we played eventually became "You Enjoy Myself," "Harry Hood," and "Dog Log." Two days before we returned home, we were jamming in front of the Pompidou museum in Paris with dozens of people dancing around us. When the bars closed, a lot more people arrived, and this incredible scene ultimately collapsed into a full-fledged riot while we kept right on playing. We made a single cassette of our music during our two months over there. The erase head on our tape recorder didn't work, but the record head did, so we overtracked everything we did into one amazing sonic collage. Unfortunately, during the Pompidou escapade someone stole my pack containing the tape.

Page: Brian Long used to come out and dance to the band when no one else would. He was good friends with a guy name Rickie Puffer, who went to Goddard. I talked to Mike about hooking up with Phish when the group played Goddard's spring fest in 1985 but had a real hard time getting in touch with them. Rickie and Brian eventually got me Mike's phone number, but if it had been a week later, I probably would have moved away and never connected with them.

Trey: When Fish, Pete, and I went to Corfu, Greece, during the summer of '85, we had to climb down a cliff to get to Pelekas Beach. Once we did, we found ourselves in a nude-beach paradise. There were tents and bamboo huts and people who had traveled from all over the world. The three of us cut down some bamboo, dried it, and built a hut we lived in for about three weeks. We befriended two insane German guys named Jürgen and Rudi, who shared some very clean LSD with us. For three weeks we drank, tripped, and enjoyed the bonfires that lined the beach every night. Some Greek punks hung a mannequin with a hard-on above a huge fire, which resembled a direct passage to hell.

There was a raft moored about a quarter to a third of a mile offshore. It took me a week to get into shape, but one day, after taking some of Jürgen and Rudi's acid, we decided to swim to it even though a storm was arriving, the wind was blowing, and whitecaps were starting to form. We stripped, dived into the ocean! and began swimming. We swam for what seemed like hours, egging each other on. Pete got scared and turned back. "You guys are crazy," he said. "Don't mess with the ocean!" I remember watching the back of his head disappear into the waves as he swam back to shore. Fish and I continued swimming while the raft bobbed up, disappeared, and moved around in front of us. At a certain moment everything changed. We were out of our minds, but we weren't joking around anymore: It was a life-or-death situation. Every muscle I had was exhausted. I went underwater and thought, "Hey, this isn't so bad." But something deep inside me made me swim back up. Fish finally made it to the raft, which was bucking up and down in the waves. He grabbed my arm and pulled me up onto the raft.

It didn't take long to realize we were probably going to die of exposure anyway. We ripped off the tarp that covered the raft and crawled under it, freezing and naked, while the wind blew and the rain fell. After a while we decided that diving back into the waves and trying to swim back to shore was a better bet than staying on the raft, and it actually was easier than swimming out. The storm blew over just as we crawled onto the beach. The dunes were flattened, the bamboo huts were blown over, and it didn't rain again. That same day I sat down with my acoustic guitar and wrote the music to "Harry Hood."

Mike: The predictably climactic "Hood" jam often sounds too New Agey for me but, depending on how hooked-up we are, it can transcend itself. Just the fact that it's happening doesn't always get me off.

Trey: The "Hood" jam is a three-chord major-key jam, but you can always take these things as far out as you want. What interests me are the different ways we can dig into it. One way is to explore tones that aren't scale notes by playing nondiatonically. Another way was pioneered by John Coltrane. At first Coltrane followed chord changes like any other jazz saxophonist, but later on he would play around a tonal center by exploring a long series of related chords by means of his awesome arpeggios, which are a chord's scale tones played in succession. I've been trying to do that more in my playing too.

Page: Across the street from the red house was a big picture of Harry Hood on the side of a two-story milk vat. It's still there. I always assumed the song concerned what happens to the little guy on the milk carton when you shut the refrigerator door on him and the light goes off.

Trey: Goddard was an insane asylum. Our gigs there, especially the Halloween shows we played between 1986 and '89, had a major influence on our ongoing scene. We usually played all night in the Sculpture Building, a space with hinged walls that crashed when you leaned up against them. There were no cops or authority figures of any kind around, and we've tried to replicate that part of the experience—on a much larger scale—at the Clifford Ball and the Great Went.

Mike: I had my peak musical experience of all time during a gig at Goddard College in November 1985. At the time I was an engineering student pondering a transfer to film. I'd just completed a se-

ABOVE, TOP TO BOTTOM: Great Went installations: Oversize clothing hangs from the stage over the crowd; bubble house; wind-sock gloves.
OPPOSITE: Fish in the Swiss-cheese house, the Great Went

ries of tests, and the pressure was temporarily off me. The entire week was a peak experience of sorts. I'd played jazz bass solos for the first time in my life during an open-mike gig with [Jazz Mandolin Project leader] Jamie Masefield, the night before our Goddard cafeteria dance. The snow had just fallen for the first time that fall the night we played, but it was still fairly warm outside. Located out in the middle of the woods, Goddard was something of an anti-institution at the time. Only about fifty people were on campus the night we played, and of the ten people who came to the dance, eight left after the first set. This was an official college event, so not coming definitely made some sort of statement.

We set up in the school cafeteria, part of which consisted of one of those circular rooms in which you can hear whispers traveling around the walls. Jeff was still in the band, and we all faced each other in a circle. We were playing two kinds of gigs at the time: either loose gigs with great jams or tight gigs where we got the changes right—but never at the same time. Our light show consisted of one red floodlight, one yellow flood, and one green flood. A couple of band members began playing while we were still setting them up, and I knew even before picking up my instrument that this gig would be infinitely tight and loose at the same time. The sun was setting, and it looked perfectly white and tranquil outside. During the first set we played "Wild Thing" and a few other songs that had been scrawled on the blackboard we set up for requests.

We went out into the hallway and passed a joint around with some strange people after the first set. I got really, *really* high, and as the rest of the band returned to the cafeteria, I realized I couldn't stand up. When I finally did, I just sort of glided like a hovercraft back downstairs. Jeff was playing

142

volume swells on his guitar, which I thought was the most incredible sound I'd ever heard. We turned off all the lights, and I started jumping up and down with the beat, not caring how I looked for perhaps the first time in my entire life. As we jammed, I felt more spiritually in tune than ever before. I felt at one with the buildings, wall outlets, chandeliers, and these people I loved. As we kept jamming, my ecstatic state didn't diminish no matter how I played or what style we played in. At one point I had a vision of Trey standing beside me in white tails with a pocket watch, as though we were performing during the 1920s.

The whole experience was like viewing a huge well-lit room after having been blind. I felt completely illuminated. I decided then and there to start a journal, and I've kept one ever since. The first two volumes were completely about that experience, then they branched off to concern related experiences of life, art, and music. How do music and art help me and others to actualize ourselves? What's the formula, if there is one? What conditions make it most likely to occur?

I was more like myself that show than ever before, but I was also part of Phish, five people in a circle who seemed to hover above the forest and move slowly through the trees. I wandered into the woods after the second set and decided never to return. Yes, filmmaking was better than engineering. But film had nothing on the musical experience I'd just had, and I was afraid I'd never be able to recapture it. So why bother? When I did return, the rest of the band decided to play another set. I was terrified another set would soil my peak experience, but it turned out to be just as great! We played for hours to the two or three people listening to us in the darkness. I decided my goals in life were to live in the woods, travel around from city to city, and try to replicate the experience I'd just had as often as possible. The whole gig's on tape, but I'll probably never listen to it.

TOP: Page and longtime Phish artist Jim Pollock, the Great Went
ABOVE: Trey and Phish manager John Paluska, the Great Went

143

The band/audience sculpture
—Phish's art is mounted on
the black triangle.

The Great Went finale,
August 17, 1997

TRACKING: BEARSVILLE AGAIN

PHISH RETURNED to Bearsville on September 29 for another four days of intense studio improvising. This time around, however, the band came to Bearsville with a newly relaxed playing style, a rejuvenated appreciation of the holy groove, the comfort of not feeling obliged to perform anything other than what the moment dictated, and euphoric memories of the Gorge and the Went.

Elektra released *Slip Stitch and Pass* on October 28. An edited version of the Hamburg show the band had played on March 1, it was the band's first single-show live album and documented the "Wolfman's Brother" jam that had recalibrated the band's musical self-image. The record's cover image of a fleet-footed man on a beach unraveling a giant ball of yarn was created by Storm Thorgerson, whose classic europsych designs have graced numerous Pink Floyd, Genesis, and Led Zeppelin albums.

"Wolfman's Brother," the album's musical centerpiece, was written in 1993 but never came fully into its own onstage until its March 1 performance in the dank, crowded Markthalle in Hamburg. There, a curious mix of young American and older German fans heard and saw the band rediscover itself yet again. This "Wolfman's Brother" started out with a woozy, undulating guitar underlying lyrics that were late-night horror show on the outside yet strangely autobiographical underneath. But as soon as these preliminaries were out of the way, the band set sail into uncharted realms of groove for the next ten minutes, interacting in a manner tighter, more confident, and simply funkier than the studio track could ever suggest. Gordon and Fishman lay down a supertight foundation while Anastasio and McConnell (mostly playing clavinet) bobbed and weaved on the surface, dipping in and out of the rhythm section's fluid pool. Music both burning in the moment and dipped in the candle wax of band history, this jam was an unmistakable high point amid an ongoing our-way musical conversation extending a dozen years into the past and paying off now in triple gold bars before decelerating slowly into the chunky white blues of ZZ Top's "Jesus Just Left Chicago." Much of that evening's music ended up on the album *Slip Stitch and Pass*, a title consisting, appropriately enough, of knitting terms. Like needles weaving a single thread into a sweater, Phish braid four musical voices into a solid yet lilting unity.

The question now was: Could the new groove be captured in the studio?

Page: We set up for our second Bearsville Studio jams in Studio A, which meant I played in the big room with everybody else rather than the isolation room I'd played in first time around. The other major difference between the two sessions was that we got into more cool grooves and textures this time. Not to say there weren't cool grooves in the first one, only fewer. We ended up with a similar amount of potential material, which Mike and I listened to most thoroughly. When the two of us got together to compare notes, we discovered we liked exactly the same things, almost to the second. Mike and I edited down the twenty hours we'd recorded to about an hour and twenty minutes, which I arranged chronologically and played for the band. Then we picked about sixteen tracks that were our favorites.

Mike: We ended up with about eight really solid grooves. We eventually want to do something with all of them, but in the meantime we thought, "What the hell, they're good grooves. We're learning all these James Brown grooves, why not learn some Phish grooves?" "Black-Eyed Katie" was something Trey came up with that jumped right out at us. But there were a few others I wish we still played, too.

Fish soloes on trombone, Aspen Mining Company, Aspen, Colorado, August 6, 1988

Page: "Black-Eyed Katie" was literally the first thing we played when we sat down and plugged in for the second Bearsville session. It was the only thing from either session we played on the fall tour. It started as a groove in one key, then we made it modulate two or three times in a James Brownish sort of way after little drum or bass breaks.

A lot of the second session consisted of cool grooves that would go for a couple of minutes and then morph into something else. Everything seemed natural and organic. The jams felt different than songs Trey and Tom have written, or even something we all wrote together, like "Tweezer," which began with a bass line and then had stuff added to it. "Black-Eyed Katie" didn't start with anything. It just happened while we were jamming and no one was paying attention.

Trey: Our recording schedule this year embraced a philosophy of nothingness. We went into the studio with nothing and nobody except John Siket and just jammed. Tom and I wrote "Ghost" and some of the other songs we played during the summer, which must have unconsciously inspired "Black-Eyed Katie." These studio sessions were completely unlike anything we'd ever done before.

THE AMERICAN RECORD industry has traditionally had difficulty accommodating bands that come onboard with a substantial audience already established over a period of time. Standard industry procedure entails signing a band that may as yet be only a local rumor, having them record an album in hopes of it yielding a radio hit, then investing money in videos and tours with the goal of creating an audience for the promising unknowns.

Phish, however, already possessed a healthy following when they signed with Elektra Records in 1991. Their audience discovered the band mainly through that greatest of all marketing tools: word of mouth generated by Phish's arduous touring schedule. Along the way the band accumulated a mailing list of fans who were kept informed of the band's activities through newsletters—first the *Phish Update* and, since 1994, *The Döniac Schvice*, currently edited by Dionysian's Jason Colton. In 1991, ardent fans Shelly Culbertson and Matt Laurence began organizing the Phishnet, the online combination of Usenet newsgroup (rec.music.phish) and website (www.phish.net) that organized fans into a loose electronic community; Phish's management also maintains the website www.phish.com. Hired by John Paluska in 1993, Culbertson, in addition to her Internet work, also runs Phish's mail-order ticket service.

Phish embraced the do-it-yourself aesthetic pioneered by punk-rock nation by independently recording and distributing their first album, *Junta*, which was released in 1988 and still vibrates with the glee of inventive young musicians discovering the recording studio's infinite potential. Phish's second album, the even more musically precocious *Lawn Boy*, was released in 1990 on the indie label Absolute-A-Go-Go and distributed by Rough Trade, which stiffed the band for an estimated $10,000 of sales when it went bankrupt the following year. The problem of distributing their music to a national audience had much to do with the band's decision to sign with Elektra Records, which released *A Picture of Nectar*—a stylistically diverse collection of hard rock, folk music, soft rock, bop, acid rock, bluegrass, country rock, calypso, and jazz-rock fusion—in 1992.

The pendulum swung in the other direction with *Rift*, a thematically coherent exploration of romantic ambivalence, which was released in 1993. The following year's *Hoist* (whose recording sessions Mike Gordon documented on his *Tracking* video) was arguably the band's most accessible album to date, and consisted of well-crafted songs that eventually came to life onstage, several interesting guest performances, and even a couple of modest radio hits. *A Live One*, released in 1995, was a generous double-CD package containing a dozen arresting live tracks distilled from the band's 1994 tours.

DeCordova
Museum, Lincoln,
Massachusetts,
May 16, 1995

Fish: *Junta* was definitely intended to be a "real" album on a real low budget. We couldn't afford much studio time, so we were mainly concerned with documenting songs before they grew too old. I think "Esther" is a great *Junta* moment. It sounds wonderful. Later we won some free recording time by competing in a battle of the bands that ended with me standing onstage, naked, holding a vacuum cleaner someone had neglected to plug in. We used our prize to record "Bathtub Gin" and "Split Open and Melt," which inspired us to write some more songs and make *Lawn Boy. A Picture of Nectar* has a few good moments but was basically a fragmented collection of all the different styles influencing us at the time. *Rift* was our attempt at a musically ambitious concept album, and came out pretty well, if a little long and cerebral.

We called our live album *A Live One* because we couldn't decide on anything else. I personally can't imagine a lamer title for a live album, and if I didn't like Phish to begin with, I think it would give me all the ammo I'd ever need to fucking hate us. We almost called it *Spontaneous Woo,* with a picture of a crazy martial artist jump kicking the camera.

Billy Breathes was an introspective record that got the title it deserved. *Billy Breathes* breathes as an album. It's as though Billy was a fictional stand-in for the band—and he's finally taking a breather.

Mike: Everyone else in the band wanted *A Live One* to have a different sound than I did. They seemed to like jams that were messy but strong, like whipping up a soup or throwing everything into a pile and letting it blend together. Tracks the others liked often sounded mushy to me. Trey loves recording ambiguous and abstract background sounds that barely register consciously. When we recorded "Strange Design" for *Billy Breathes* (although we decided to leave it off at the last minute), he produced mouth noises just soft enough so you don't necessarily hear them consciously. I'm a big fan of Jerry Garcia's recording philosophy. He liked to hear each note distinctly, which is why he gravitated toward the banjo.

Trey: Rather than representing the best music we make during a particular era, our live albums seem to document transitional moments. So *A Live One* has the Bangor "Tweezer" and the Great Woods "Stash" [7/8/94], which is the oldest thing on the album. Other "Stash"s might have been better, but that's the one we really took over the top in that kind of frantic way we were playing back then. And the "Wilson" [12/30/94] was either the first or second time the chanting thing happened.

Mike: I thought we flew into a rhythmic time warp for a moment while we were recording "Stash" for *A Picture of Nectar*. Not only were we really jamming in the studio for the first time, but those ten seconds were definitely the best thing we'd ever recorded. I said, "Wasn't that a great take? Let's keep it." Everyone agreed, but Trey, who was in the habit of constantly improving his guitar parts by recording over them—something he was very good at—said, "I'm just going to give it one pass on the guitar." I got mad and begged him to leave the one section we all hooked up on, and he agreed. I went away for an hour. When I came back, Trey said, "I tried some other solos but everyone agrees the original is the best, except for this one little section." I said, "Fine, as long as it's not the one section I asked you not to change." It turned out that the ten seconds I'd really liked were the ten seconds he'd erased and replaced. We had a big argument—crying and everything. The engineer thought the new riff was cooler, but Trey finally agreed to listen to the DAT of how we'd played it originally. Then, while I went away again, he reproduced it verbatim. The fact that he'd changed it, and then changed it back, made it even more special to me.

Fish: Part of our growth process consists in reaching certain milestones where we realize it's time for a change. We've definitely transcended the lowest-common-denominator part of our career, the *Hoist/Live One* era when all four of us were concerned with growth, popularity, and trying to please everybody. That resulted in a safety zone and not having as much fun as we used to.

Hoist should have been called *Herschel the Owl,* or *I Heard the Owl Herscheling.* Herschel the Owl was in this great series of nature photographs you can see Trey and me cracking up over in Mike's *Tracking* video. First you see a tree line. A little closer in you see two small yellow dots. Next you see this tiny owl sitting on a branch, then a picture of the funniest owl face ever. We looked into acquiring the rights to use it for the album cover, but chickened out and hired the artist who ended up photographing Amy Skelton's suspended horse, Maggie. It boiled down to our fear of coming off as stupid. At the time there was an organization-wide concern with our being construed as too silly. We traditionally do our thing, the argument went, then stick our collective foot in our mouth by doing something ridiculous. I was never totally on the bandwagon with that one.

The *Billy Breathes* cover decision, on the other hand, took two seconds. Someone held up a picture Mike had taken of himself and said, "Let's use this." Done. In retrospect, maybe we overcompensated. The path to a good album cover probably lies somewhere in the middle.

Page: We didn't play most of the songs on *Hoist* before we recorded them because someone in Elektra's upper management theorized we weren't selling albums because everybody had already heard the songs on them. It wasn't a bad idea, just wrong. But it gave us an opportunity to let songs come together in the studio without our preconceiving them onstage.

Fish: In an attempt to both maintain our integrity as well as a good working relationship with Elektra Records, we invited the producer into the songwriting process when we recorded *Hoist.* It wasn't easy. Certain people in the company may actually appreciate our music, but they also have

Fish fixes himself a bite during the *Hoist* recording sessions, American Studios, Woodland Hills, California, November 1993.

an eye on their job, which is to make money from what we do. With *Hoist* we decided to embrace the process. Both we and Elektra wanted to have something on the radio, so we tried to write a hit single. But we never committed ourselves to it totally. We had one foot in the door, but another part of us was too self-consciously afraid of self-betrayal to go for it completely. *Hoist* maintains most of its musical integrity, but "Down with Disease" simply sucks. It left a bad taste in my mouth for a long time, and it's taken years for me not to regard lines like "a thousand barefoot children dancing on my lawn" and "this has all been wonderful, but now I'm on my way" as whiningly cynical. And I wanted to kill myself after "Dog Faced Boy."

Page: We loosened up a lot more on *Hoist* than we had on our earlier studio projects. *Rift* was ambitious, conceptual, wild, and big. We had a lot of complicated music but no time to record it. *Hoist* was lighter and more fun. It was definitely a turning point, and as consciously commercial an album as we had ever made. All our songs take time to mature. They never really come into their own until after the albums are out and all the hype about them has died down.

Tom: *Hoist* was Trey's and my big telephone-songwriting album. I had a new baby and no time or money to spend writing with Trey in person. Also, the band was touring heavily prior to recording in Los Angeles in fall '93, and I never made it out there. Phish was a separate entity from me entirely at that point. Trey and I were close pals and everything, but we rarely hung out. During *Rift* and *Hoist* we'd only see each other at shows and have conversations like, "Hey, how's it going? Here are five new lyrics." When the band started making more money, there were spare hotel rooms for people like me to join them on tour. It enabled us to hang out more, which was great.

Fish: Paul Fox, our producer on *Hoist,* had just come off 10,000 Maniacs' *Our Time in Eden,* which sold millions of copies. We were supposed to be the next band he broke.

Trey: I wrote "If I Could" in about five minutes after a heart-to-heart talk with the usually cheerful Amy Skelton, who was very depressed about something at the time. It was one of those songs that emerged spontaneously. It was pretty different from what I'd been writing until then, and was probably a bit of an eyebrow raiser for some of our audience. But hey, I got to sing a duet with Alison Krauss, so I can die happy.

Tom: Despite being a blatant crowd pleaser, "Sample in a Jar" is one of my favorite songs. My boss at the Educational Testing Service had a wonderfully strange sense of humor. Driving in his car one day, we passed a nice-looking black guy on the side of the road and went off on a long riff about him. We decided he was named Leemor—Leemor LeLift. I used my friend Dave's father, Elihu, because I needed a three-syllable name, and his is a particularly cool one. Plus, I wanted to use every member of Dave's family in a song. His mother's name is Guelah, while Dave himself is the Dave of "looks too much like Dave" fame. His brother, John, has yet to be immortalized.

Page: We were in Los Angeles working on drum sounds toward the end of the first *Hoist* recording session. Paul Fox and Ed Thacker had more or less finished miking the drums and they said, "Let's run a track to make sure we're getting everything." I think we chose "Sample" because it's nice to start with something easy, as in basic. We pretty much nailed it first take. I walked into the control room after we finished playing it, and Paul said, "Sounds like a record to me," which is what you say when you make a CD these days.

Tom: The last line, before the final chorus, used to be, "The friendly skies and good times seem all wrong." It referred to a former boss who took me for a ride in his plane and later hit on me, thus making it impossible for me to stay at that particular job. I wrote about *his* boss, incidentally, in "Buffalo Bill."

Trey: The first line means something different every time we play it: "It's hidden far away / But someday I may tell / The tale of mental tangle / When into your world I fell." You could be talking to your friend, lover, audience, anybody. "Sample" is basically about sitting in a car with the seat belt on, drunk.

Page: "Sample" contains a catchy little progression not unreminiscent of Status Quo's "Pictures of Matchstick Men."

Tom: "Down with Disease" is pure documentary. I had mononucleosis and actually felt pretty great in a run-down way. I had a lot of fun hanging around my apartment, but the demons came out at night and gave me some horrible dreams. When I have bad dreams, which isn't all that often, I usually wake up and think, "That was really cool." But with mono I'd wake up and not want to go back to sleep because the evil imagery would return immediately. Trey added the "nothing I can say to make it stop" line.

Page: "Down with Disease" and "Simple" evolved into big jam songs during fall '96. When we first played "Down with Disease" live, it was hard to leave its five-chord progression. When we play it now, though, we generally hang on A-major with a flatted seventh, and sometimes go down to G. Then Trey plays the riff, and we finish it. But once Fish learned to leave the beat, and Mike and I escaped the chord progression once or twice, we figured it out.

Fish: For a long time the lyrics to "Down with Disease" seemed a little cynical to me. "A thousand barefoot children dancing on my lawn" sounded like a big complaint to me, and we're four of the happiest people on earth, so what the fuck were we complaining about? But it wasn't the song's fault we made a blatant stab at bogus commercialism when we recorded and made a video of it.

Trey: Tom certainly wasn't writing about being famous. "Waiting for the time when I can finally say / That this has all been wonderful, but now I'm on my way" is universal.

Mike: I enjoyed making the "Down with Disease" video, although the rest of the band disliked both the process and end result, which I'm not wild about either. The band argued for years about whether or not to make a video, and I was the only one who definitely wanted to. I didn't mind the idea of us becoming more popular or exposing our music to more people, and I didn't have anything against MTV like they did, probably because I'd never really watched it and hadn't seen many rock videos. So I ended up renting an office in South Boston and played director. It took two days to shoot, much of which was spent hanging from the ceiling on thin wires that dug painfully into our thighs. I found it relaxing, even cathartic, dangling up there, but the other guys hated it. Their main complaint when it was all over was that there wasn't enough of my personality in the video.

Tom: I wonder how many people used "This has all been wonderful, but now I'm on my way" as their high school yearbook quote?

Trey: Mike became hyperanalytic about his vocal when we cut "Scent of a Mule." He spent an entire day trying out different inflections. Page and I finally went out and bought a bottle of Wild Turkey, brought it back to the studio, and said, "Why don't you try this?" Mike was game. He drank it down, got a great take, then passed out on the couch.

ABOVE: Bearsville Studios, May 1996
OPPOSITE: Outside the Barn, Bearsville Studios, May 1996

Tom: A frightening thing happened while Phish was recording "Julius" in Los Angeles. Trey wanted some words to go with the swing riff at the end, so I gave him "Before you take another step / Don't blame it on yourself / 'Cause if you lay it on a brother when he's sleeping, / Wake up in the morning you'll be gone" over the phone. He asked me what they meant, and I said, "I don't think they mean anything." He laughed and said, "Well, you'd better think something up." As it turned out, the Rickey Grundy Chorale, a black gospel choir from Los Angeles they'd hired for the track, refused to sing "Julius" until they knew what it meant. The "lay it on a brother" part apparently gave them problems. I wasn't home when someone from the studio called me to explain it, and I'm glad I wasn't. Trey phoned later to say he'd made something up and they'd bought it. I probably would have put my foot in my mouth, because I still don't know what it means other than demonstrating my ignorance of Roman history.

Trey: I was in the vocal booth while the lead singer from the Rickey Grundy Chorale sang her amazing "Julius" solo. When she was done, she looked right at me and pointed like, "Now you sing." I laughed so hard my headphones fell off.

Mike: I brought my four-track version of "Simple" to the *Hoist* sessions along with a few other songs. At that time it sounded like Simon and Garfunkel doing a fifties song, and Paul Fox didn't like it.

THOUGH IT STARTED out as a rickety country number that was left off of *Hoist*, "Simple" eventually evolved into as anthemic and elegant a description of the band and its audience as could be imagined. It's also the Phish song Tom Marshall says he would have most liked to have written himself.

Fish: "Simple" makes me really happy to be part of the band that wrote it. We knew Mike's original version of "Simple" was a great song from the start, but it was too countryish or bluegrassy to do onstage. It made me think of a rickety cart rolling down a road.

Mike: Trey misheard the first line, so we ended up changing "We've got cymbals" to "We've got it simple." After forgetting about it for a while, I started singing the words to "Simple" while we were jamming "Mike's Song" in Eugene, Oregon [5/12/94]. It sounded anthemic—maybe a little too anthemic for some people. Several of our songs have fairly undefined bass lines, and this is one of them.

"Weekapaug Groove" used to be slower and funkier when we first played it, and my hand didn't get so tired slapping it out. Then it got really fast and became impossible to keep up with. Now it's reached a happy medium in terms of rhythm. The faster beat was easier on Trey but harder for me to loosen up to. I remember thinking when I wrote "Mike's Song"—although I hardly consider it a song—that we had too many major-key jams and needed a minor one. I basically stole the minor part from Ted Nugent's "Stranglehold." I recently added another downbeat in the bass line to fatten it up.

Page: Our "Mike's Song" jams have morphed over the years. "Simple" is in F. The "Mike's Song" jam is mainly in F-sharp, although for the past three or four years we've modulated it a half step lower. When we used to play it with Trey and Mike on the trampolines, they'd both turn around halfway through the jam, and we'd bring it down a half step.

One of the first and best times we played "Simple" was in Milwaukee's Eagles Ballroom the night O. J. Simpson went on the lam in his white Bronco [6/17/94]. We sang, "We've got O.J., because we've got a band," among other things.

Mike: Not all our rituals take place onstage. We performed our first Oh Kee Pa ceremony at Trey's tiny apartment under the Lickety Split restaurant in Plainfield, where he lived like a troll on the riverbank. The ceremony itself involved drinking hot chocolate made with vanilla, maple syrup, fresh chocolate, and a half-ounce of marijuana. Then we played nonstop for eight to ten hours, including our first "Weekapaug Groove." Trey got the idea for the Oh Kee Pa ceremonies from the film *A Man Called Horse* and the book *Modern Primitives*.

Trey: I remember Fish lying motionless with his head on a snare drum for about four hours while the three of us played during one Oh Kee Pa ceremony. And I recall Mike closing his eyes and playing one note really loudly for a couple of hours at another. We actually left the room for about half an hour to get a drink. When we came back he was still going. He never even knew we were gone.

Mike: We held our second Oh Kee Pa ceremony in our practice room at Paul Languedoc's house. Trey lit candles everywhere and we recorded onto an eight-track tape machine. The version of "Union Federal" on *Junta* came out of that session. Paul thought it was the stupidest thing he'd ever seen, but I loved it. The sound quality we got from the two cheap microphones hanging from the ceiling onto a lousy tape deck was much better than what we usually get in the studio.

    The closest thing we've done to an Oh Kee Pa ceremony recently was the flatbed-truck jam we did in the middle of the Clifford Ball, late at night. Everything was really dreamy, Fish's ride cymbal kept everybody afloat, and we all pulsated together in varying relationships to the beat.

Fish: "Simple" is probably my favorite song in our entire repertoire, and the "Simple" riff is the

RIGHT: Bearsville Studios, May 1996
OPPOSITE, LEFT TO RIGHT: Page, Fish, producer Steve Lillywhite, engineer Jon Siket, Trey, engineer Chris Laidlaw, and Mike, Bearsville Studios, May 1996

best riff in Trey's mighty arsenal of riffs. It's so great he can play it through the entire song without anyone getting sick of it.

Page: Even though we came up with the arrangement together, "Simple" was definitely Mike's tune in terms of lyrics and melody. Trey sometimes gives us credit for songs he's written as much as Mike wrote this one, and we've all made contributions to the Marshall/Anastasio songs along the way. But on occasion Trey will generously say, "Let's call it a band composition," even though I might not have had any more to do with that song than I did with another one. He doesn't have to do it, but it's a nice gesture.

ABOVE: Phish manager John Paluska, Bearsville Studios, May 1996

Fish: The reason I sing "We've got skyscraper" with tongue so firmly in cheek is that we never set out to find a record company. I enjoy the benefits of having a record company, but I especially appreciate the fact that we've now earned enough money so that if Elektra doesn't want to put something of ours out, they don't have to, and I don't have to worry about paying my bills.

THE BAND BEGAN the *Billy Breathes* sessions at Bearsville Studios on their own in February 1996, without yet having hired a producer. Their first order of business was the mad-scientist creation of the "Blob." Steve Lillywhite joined them midway through the four-month recording process, sifting through the preceding months' work and reorganizing it into what is arguably the band's most accessibly artful recording. Downright organic in comparison to its predecessors, the latter half of *Billy Breathes*, especially, flows like a single ongoing work slightly reminiscent of the second side of the Beatles' *Abbey Road*. Relatively quiet and rustic compared to other Phish albums, *Billy Breathes* reflects both the rural Burlington outskirts in which the band resides as well as the Bearsville barn in which it was recorded. Warm, if not fuzzy, and lyrically contradictory—some songs reflect the band's celebrity; others celebrate Anastasio's recent fatherhood—the album is an honest if ambivalent declaration of hope and frustration parceled out in relatively concise and radio-amiable songs that also include a couple of outright rockers.

Page: The Blob was an experiment we invented to loosen us up in the studio for *Billy Breathes*—the same way the "Hey" exercises loosen us up for playing onstage. First we drew straws and recorded one note at a time in rotation. Then we took turns *removing* notes from the tape. This taught us not to get overly attached to our contributions, because another band member could always erase them. In the past we've always had a limited amount of studio time, which has its own benefits. When our engineer showed up, he thought we'd probably want to set up and jam for a while. Little did he know we'd request three huge marker boards for a grid detailing what the Blob contained. Between the three and three-and-a-half-minute marks, for example, the entire band jammed on tracks fifteen and sixteen, with twenty seconds of bowed bass on another track. It wasn't just vocals on one track and kick drum on another. We played all the instruments we could: Mellotron for ten seconds here, vibes for two seconds there. Whenever we wanted to tape something, we'd have to look for space to fit it in. So we went around in a circle for about two weeks, and the music that became "Steep" came right out of the middle.

Trey: Steve Lillywhite went right into *Billy Breathes* without ever having met us, heard our albums, or seen us play live. We called him up four days before we went back into the studio following a break. He'd heard about us from Dave Matthews, and he got around to listening to *Rift* about three weeks into the project. He didn't like it much. After we finished the album, he finally saw us live in London and was like, "Let's do it again!" He had no idea what we were really like.

Fish: When we recorded *Rift,* we were control freaks who tied Barry Beckett's hands. The one song we let him go to town on—"Fast Enough For You"—is the best-sounding thing on the album. Barry just wasn't up for fighting with us all the time.

Mike: While we were recording *Billy Breathes* I spent hours a day in the control room on the Internet, mainly convincing people in chat rooms that it was really me. I liked being quizzed. Someone asked, "If you're Mike, what are the chords to 'Fee'?" And I couldn't remember a single chord. Somebody else asked, "If you're Mike, how long is Trey's hair right now?" I'd been with Trey for twelve hours a day for two months, and I couldn't tell you if his hair was short, crewcut, or long. I failed the test.

Tom: I brought thirty or forty poems to the Cayman Islands when Trey and I vacationed there in February 1996. Trey always says *Billy Breathes* is a slow, acoustic album because we went to the islands with only an acoustic guitar and bongos. We called the Cayman Islands song-demo tape we made *King Cayman Beluga,* and much of it ended up on *Billy Breathes.* We experimented with switching lyrics and music around, which eventually made the lyrical repetitions of "Swept Away," "Steep," and "Character Zero" seem natural.

Mike: The *Billy Breathes* version of "Character Zero" is just a big pile of energy. Certain sections of the groove sound fine to me, but overall it sounds a little empty. When Trey brought it to the studio, Page hated it. He thought it sounded vapid next to everything else on the album. But everyone finally liked it in the end, especially Steve Lillywhite. He always cranked it up really loud in the control room.

Tom: The first part of "Character Zero" was originally a poem I wrote called "Convince." The only thing we added was, "I oughtta see the man Mulcahey." Trey and I had a blast buzzing around the Caymans in our rented Suzuki four-wheel-drive convertible. Trey always drove, and I always operated the radio. One night we heard this hilariously fucked-up Jamaican DJ and started screaming along to him, "I-I oughtta sleep now Mulcahey." It was very cathartic at the time.

Page: "Character Zero" is a three-chord rock song—nothing more, nothing less—and I wasn't initially in favor of putting it on *Billy Breathes.* It's basically a funny, dumb rock song—which isn't a put-down. It's not easy to write a good little rock song. But I felt it didn't mesh with the energy or mood of what we'd recorded prior to Lillywhite's arrival. The album changed a lot after Steve came along. We recorded "Taste," "Cars Trucks Buses," and "Zero," not to mention redoing the end of the album with him. Now I'm glad it made the cut because it adds excitement and makes a nice transition after "Free."

Trey: Lillywhite showed up a couple of weeks after we recorded a demo version of "Character Zero," and he jumped all over it. It was a little heavy-handed for my taste, but he really liked its energy, so we added vocals to it. I spent a lot of time working on the album's sequence, and "Zero" kept jumping out at me as I drove around in my car listening to what we had and thinking about how it should flow. Steve definitely wanted it to be the first or second track, to kick off the album with a bang. Personally, I think the second half of the album is much better than the first.

Page: I wrote "Cars Trucks Buses" for my friend Rusty Martin's twisted movie, *Only in America*.

ABOVE: Marley, Bearsville Studios, May 1996
OPPOSITE: Mike and childhood friend Rebecca Kolodny recording a Store 24 commercial—Mike's first studio experience—as his father, Bob Gordon, looks on, 1974

Mike: We added "Cars Trucks Buses," which I've always liked, during the second half of the *Billy Breathes* sessions. I remember being bummed out that my song, "Weekly Time," didn't make the cut. It failed when I sang it. But "Cars Trucks Buses" added a funk element to the album and wasn't by Trey, so it mixed the album up a little more.

Fish: Page told me he wanted a drum part that could fade in and out of the train sound that bracketed the song on the sound track.

Mike: "Cars Trucks Buses" began as a butt-kicking funk number. We almost turned it into a typically busy Phish song by layering on a high-pitched cowbell and a wind sound you can barely hear. When I brought this up, we ended up holding off on some of these sounds until the third chorus, and spaced them out more.

Tom: When we first fooled around with what became "Waste," Trey and I made up lines like, "Don't want to be a hammer," "Don't want to be a toaster," and other crap. In the Caymans I was more interested in the lyrics I'd already written than in coming up with new words. But Trey kept saying, "This is either going to be great or horribly cheesy." In fact, on the original tape Trey says, "This is going to be a joke, but let's do it anyway." We sang it, went to dinner, came back, and fell in love with it.

Mike: "Train Song" was originally part of the Blob. At one point I invited Trey to my room to discuss the song. He had some clear ideas about the lyrics—he's had so much experience writing songs—and reshaped the whole tune into a concise story. He played his pocket change while I played guitar and sang, and we recorded the new version on a minicassette. Then I called my friend Joe Linitz, who had written the original poem, and he wrote some new lyrics about getting off the train and walking into a house. When we recorded it, Trey played his pocket change again, I played guitar, Fish played vibraphone, and Page added bowed acoustic bass. To be honest, it could have sounded better. My voice cracked a couple of times, which bugged me, but the rest of the band encouraged me to keep it in. They called it the "hillbilly crack."

Fish: We each had about two minutes to do something on the Blob. I heard something for piano in my head when it was my turn. I recorded half the phrase that ended up on "Swept Away," and was floundering around looking for the two notes to complete it when Trey said, "Time's up." Then he went out and immediately finished the riff with the exact two notes I'd been looking for. I didn't mention it at the time because I was so blown away by our little telepathic moment.

Trey: "Swept Away" started off peppier, like Gladys Knight and the Pips, when Tom and I wrote it in the Caymans. I ended up sticking the melody and words on a piece of the Blob.

Though we never intended it, *Billy Breathes* ended up having a nice back-to-the-water theme. It opens with "Free," which contains the line, "In a minute I'll be free, and you'll be splashing in the sea." The album winds up with lines like "Till I'm finally swept away," "Riverbanks will soon erode in canyons that have overflowed," and a section that sounds like mud and water. And then "O! to be Prince Caspian, afloat upon the waves."

Mike: "Swept Away" needs a bass line.

Trey: We'd been up all night and the sun was rising when we recorded the jam that begins "Prince Caspian" on *Billy Breathes.* The song meandered endlessly before Steve Lillywhite got his hands on it. He edited the beginning of one take to the end of another. Steve gave the song form out of my strumming two chords for fifteen minutes before we added lyrics. He also created the ending. I hate to give away our trade secrets, but it's an edit. Two pieces of tape Scotch-taped together and looped.

Fish: Like a lot of songs, "Prince Caspian" came together only after we'd exhausted the thinking process. Most of the time we write a song, learn to play it, then obsess about it. We'll play it one way one night, another way another night, discuss it among ourselves, ask other people about it, decide it's this and not that, or try to force it to be something it isn't. Finally one day we'll get so damn tired of analyzing it, we just go out and play it with a *fuck this* attitude—and it usually ends up sounding great.

Trey: "Prince Caspian" was inspired by seeing Neil Young and Crazy Horse in France. A two-chord Crazy Horse jam is no less transcendent than anyone else's note-filled extravaganza. But for us to pull it off, everyone has to abandon themselves to the frenzy; we need to play in the mode of the Velvet Underground's live album *1969*. In fact, the first time Jeff Holdsworth, Fish, Mike, and I played together as Phish—in the Wing Hall dorm lounge at UVM—all Jeff and I did was strum two chords for half an hour. I clearly remember us locking into this tight, wailing rhythm. I'd hate to think we could ever reach a point where we thought we were above belting out two chords because we knew how to play a lot of other notes.

Neil Young blazes a direct path to the soul without clogging it up with too much thought. I didn't understand him at all in high school, but the older I get, the more he speaks to me. I heard "Thrasher" recently for the first time in years. I called Tom and asked him if he'd heard it lately. "When was the last time you listened to 'The Wedge'?" he said. "It's my big secret." He sang me the verse from "Thrasher" that goes, "They had the best selection / They were poisoned with protection"—lines about friends of his who never took risks and now look at them. But Tom continued with "I'm building you a pyramid / With limestone blocks so large / I dragged them from the mountaintop / You'll need a two-car garage." He told me that he wrote three more verses to "Thrasher" during a fifteen-mile bike ride, sent them to me, and I set them to a completely different rhyme scheme and rhythm in "Wedge."

Page: We were just fooling around, concluding a not-very-good "Caspian" take by thrashing on our instruments. We ended up looping a couple of measures long enough to fade out on.

Fish: *Billy Breathes* taught us how to record an album. We finally realized that a recording studio was more than a place to try to reproduce what we did onstage. For years we'd been mistakenly attempting to translate the way we played live onto an album, and that's useless. We never tried to translate what we did on albums onto the stage, so why do the reverse? People have shorter attention spans for albums than they do for concerts. Without the atmosphere of a concert as distraction, it's just you and the audio input. So things need to move along to maintain your attention. If you want to put a long jam on your record, it had better be something damn good that goes someplace interesting. There's more leeway to develop ideas during a concert. A record is like a sculpture. You start off with a big pile of stuff and edit it down to something permanent. A show, on the other hand, is of the moment.

Page: After debuting "Taste" in Boise [6/7/95], we took it back to the practice room and really reworked it with entirely different lyrics. Then we wrote "The Fog That Surrounds," as sung by Fish, over exactly the same chord progression. We played that for a while, to mixed reviews, then brought it back to the practice room at least one more time until we finally took the best part of "The Fog That Surrounds," Fish's middle break, and stuck it into "Taste." Then we put the piano solo—I get to play over the chord changes jazz style—in front of the big droning D-major jam. "Taste" ended up being a breakthrough for us.

During the *Billy Breathes* session we recorded something called "Taken Far Away," which consisted of us repeating that phrase along with the "trampled by lambs and pecked by the dove" line. Once or twice during sound checks we played another song called "Chinese Wall," which included the lines "Drop me off the Chinese wall / Peel my fingers off the rim" sung to a completely different two-chord progression. So we'd actually been messing with bits and pieces of "Limb by Limb" for years until they all returned as a complete song that was so much better than those earlier things that I totally forgot about them until just now.

Bearsville Studios, May 1996

"Wading in the Velvet Sea" has that same quality of the lyrics repeating over and over again that so many of that batch do. But it does this in a softer, more ambient way, whereas "Piper" builds slowly to a frenzy, the lyrics come in, and it suddenly stops. These tunes are more like concepts than traditional songs in that they really don't have verses, choruses, A/B structures, or solos.

Tom: Phish was feeling they'd taken a wrong direction by concentrating on pieced-together Trey songs like "Fluffhead" and "Divided Sky." They wanted to refocus on tunes where the content takes you somewhere. Gibberish lyrics and jams obviously have a place in Phish, but Trey really enjoyed crafting songs like "Waste" for *Billy Breathes.*

Trey: I used to hate *Hoist.* I felt we were caving in to all the pressure on us to achieve commercial success. But now I consider it one of our better albums in many ways. Not that I'd ever put it on my CD player or anything. I don't know why, but I can't play any of our albums. I always hope I'm recording an album I could actually listen to, but that's just wishful thinking. I'll probably never think we have an album that good, because as soon as we finish it, we're beyond it. I tend to loathe anything I do for about six months after it's completed. But the *Hoist* tunes have become some of my favorites to play. "Wolfman's Brother" is definitely the highlight of *Slip Stitch and Pass.* It represents much of what I hoped Phish could be, and I didn't even notice it happening at the time.

THE STORY OF THE GHOST: FALL TOUR

BEGINNING IN mid-November, Phish played a twenty-one-date fall tour that began in Las Vegas and then Z'ed across the Midwest and the East Coast before concluding in Albany, New York. The band removed several older songs from regular rotation, replaced them with a substantial mass of new Anastasio/Marshall material, and enjoyed a newly relaxed approach to their performances. Phish made an additional adjustment early on in the tour. The result was a series of postshow set lists studded with asterisks signifying songs that either went unfinished, were extended to unusual lengths, or included unexpected teases of other tunes. Two new cover versions—the Rolling Stones' "Emotional Rescue" and Buddy Miles's "Them Changes"—and revived covers of Stevie Wonder's "Boogie On Reggae Woman" and Robert Palmer's "Sneakin' Sally Through the Alley" were funky homages that made clear the direction in which Phish was tending. Another new cover, Ween's "Roses Are Free," wouldn't fully flower until the following spring.

OPPOSITE: Load-in, Fleet Center, Boston, Massachusetts, December 30, 1996

Two shows in particular exemplified the looser (as in tighter) version of Phish that was now hitting its stride. The second of two appearances at Denver's McNichols Arena (11/17/1997) proved as significant a musical watershed as March's Hamburg appearance. And the middle of three shows (11/29/1997) played at the Worcester Centrum resulted in an hour-long "Runaway Jim," the band's lengthiest, purely instrumental onstage excursion to date, that explored island after musical island before settling down into "Strange Design."

Page: Tom and Trey got together for a couple more writing sessions and came up with songs like "This Is a Farmhouse," which we debuted on Conan O'Brien's show [11/7/97]. Then, rather than repeating the approach we took on the second Europe tour, concentrating on new material and avoiding specific older songs, we said, "No more rules. Anything goes." The most important thing became having a good time out there. The new songs were well broken in and certain material had risen to the top. We wanted to do a lot of improvising and go onstage without a set list.

Trey: The areas of risk and safety switched places between '96 and '97. One thing we did different is we instituted a new no-analyzing rule for the fall tour up through New Year's Eve. We decided we wouldn't talk about what occurred onstage between sets or after the show, and we didn't. As soon as we got offstage, that was it. Whatever happened, happened, and on to the next thing. It felt incredibly liberating to me.

Before, we'd play something like "Run Like an Antelope," come offstage, and Mike and Fish might get into an argument about whether or not the bass drum was supposed to be half-swung. But what's the point? After fifteen years are we really going to improve the way we play "Run Like an Antelope" by worrying about what Fish does with his kick drum? From now on, we decided, we'll save the criticisms for rehearsal and just have a good time on tour. And it made all the difference.

Page: We talk about our playing offstage more than most bands do, I imagine. Historically, we'll sit in the band room during the break and go through each song and what each of us may or may not have liked about it, venting and pointing fingers. The time for that should be during practice sessions, not on the road.

We didn't go on tour planning not to analyze it. It was something we came up with the second night, in Salt Lake City. Somebody said, as a joke, "God, wouldn't it be amazing if we went through a show without analyzing between sets?" And as the tour went on, somebody would start to say something between sets about how we played, and the other three of us would say, "Are you analyzing? No analyzing!" It built and built. The one show we actually did sort of analyze was not the best show of the tour—and I'm not going to tell you what it was.

Trey: Not analyzing, combined with not knowing what we were going to do until we got onstage, lent every set a sense of possibility and abandonment. We're overly self-analytic as a rule, and I constantly try to break us out of our patterns. In 1996, for example, I thought I was playing way too many guitar solos. I wanted to figure out ways to avoid so much guitar in the mix, so first I got a percussion set. Then I began to hide behind my amp and wait for Page to play more solos. Neither of those ideas worked especially well. Then, all of a sudden, lo and behold, we're playing sparse rhythmic music, the other guys are stepping forward, and I'm deeper in the mud. But I sure couldn't force that to happen. What worked was a general abandonment of preconceptions symbolized by music where we all get out of the way and simply let it pulsate.

Page: We simply relaxed and avoided going to those places that made us doubt ourselves. It was definitely a confidence builder for certain band members, and for others it was a relief to not have to listen to criticisms. So each of us benefited in our own ways.

Fish: Everybody knows when we've been playing listlessly. We've all gotten down on ourselves for

not listening as well as we're capable of. We've never just gone through the motions of a set, but if we're not interacting at our optimum, Trey would take on the role of coach, ass kicker, or bandleader, and say something like, "Every time we go out onstage, I want us to be one of the best bands out there. If we're not going to fucking play like we mean it, if we're not going to listen to each other like we know we can, what's the point of being up there?" I think it's great when he's like that. He's good at it. The few times I've attempted to take on the role, I've seemed to offend everybody.

Trey: Paul Asbell, who plays in Burlington's Unknown Blues Band, told me his group is the polar opposite of ours. In twenty years he's never been able to get anyone to talk about *anything* that happened onstage. But we managed to talk ourselves into a hole on a fairly regular basis.

Page: It ended up being maybe my favorite tour ever. We even started listening to ourselves during these parties we had on the bus. We were listening without analyzing, getting high on Phish, on ourselves. Everything was peachy keen.

TOP: Sound engineer Paul Languedoc, the Centrum, Worcester, Massachusetts, December 28, 1995 ABOVE: Paul Languedoc, Townsend Family Park, Townsend, Vermont, July 14, 1991

Trey: While the band makes and breaks rules for itself all the time, the Phish organization only has two rules. Rule number one is *Don't piss off Paul*, and many, many decisions have been made on the basis of that rule. From the caterers to the lighting people, our crew's the tightest, most professional one on the road thanks to Paul Languedoc, who was our first and only crew member when we started out. In addition to running our sound back then, Paul also built my guitar, Mike's bass, all our onstage risers, the entire monitor system, and every equipment case we used. He also drove and repaired our truck.

PAUL LANGUEDOC first met Phish in 1984 when Anastasio sold his Ibanez guitar in order to buy a new one from Time Guitars in Burlington, where Languedoc was employed as a guitar maker. The musician and luthier struck up a friendship, and a couple of years later Languedoc custom-built a hollow-body instrument Anastasio subsequently performed on for the next nine years. "Trey's a one-guitar guy," says Languedoc. Languedoc first helped with the band's sound at a Goddard College gig when they still performed through Mike Gordon's small sound system. Languedoc's first show as the band's official soundman was at Hunt's in Burlington, in October 1986, and he's been behind the sound board ever since.

Running Phish's sound system entails more than merely connecting microphones into a console that puts out a signal to the speakers. Languedoc's console sends different mixes to the main PA, front and rear "fill" speakers, and the delay speakers. Right and left mixes are equalized and compressed before entering a crossover network that splits the signals into the appropriate frequency ranges for each type of speaker. A digital-delay unit aligns by milliseconds the signals received by three sets of speakers. The band itself delivers some fifty-five signals to two different boards connected to a rack containing two dozen compressors, reverb and echo effects, and the tape decks that record every show onto forty tracks.

"What I enjoy most," Languedoc says, when asked about the art in his job, "is how every-body on our road crew works together without any power struggles. It almost sounds silly, but I think our crew epitomizes an organic management style in which everybody works together as equals. Ninety-nine percent of the time I'm just doing my job on the road—but every so often a really special connection occurs. I can tell the band knows how good they sound, the lights are completely amazing, the crowd is totally into the show, and I think, 'This is really fun!'"

Mike: Once at Nectar's a fret popped halfway off the neck of my bass during a song. Paul came on-stage with a hammer while I kept playing the other strings and whacked it back into place.

Trey: When I was twelve, I played right wing on the Lawrence junior hockey team. My dad was our coach, took it very seriously, and almost carried us to the nationals. It was frustrating at times be-cause he expected a lot from me. He was in that awkward position of coaching his son but not wanting to show favoritism, so he had to be extra hard on me. My mother is very creative and non-traditional; she travels a lot, and keeps all her belongings in one small bag. My father, on the other hand, is extremely grounded. I've learned a lot from each of them. I picked up my organizational skills and so-called leadership qualities from my father. I used to plan all our band practices days in advance and model them on hockey practice. I knew if we didn't have an agenda, our tendency would be to drink beer, smoke a joint, and sit around noodling and flipping channels for hours. In-stead, rehearsals became both focused and loose—which epitomizes Phish to a certain degree. The band is greater than the sum of its parts because we've always worked hard at maximizing our talents.

Trey and his father,
Ernie Anastasio,
1973

Fish: On a given night, any one of us might be the star player. Every once in a while somebody has to step up to the plate and kick some ass when the team's falling apart.

Trey: Phish wouldn't remotely be where we are without John Paluska, our manager. He's totally responsible for much of our success. I've seen a lot of talented bands with management problems. John is both creative and knows when to stay out of our way, even if we go down a less than brilliant road. John and Tom are probably the two most silently important people who've made Phish what it is. And since I've spent most of every day for the past five years talking to them on the phone, I should know.

Tom: I have the best job in Phish. I don't have to tour but can always hit the best shows. And I don't have to show up for sound check.

Fish: From the musicians to the crew to our managers, I never take what we have for granted. It makes me want to practice harder to up-hold my part of it.

Trey: The second night in Colorado was one of my favorite shows on the fall tour, and my favorite thing in it was the "Ghost" we played. The truly funny thing about the tour is that we actually enjoyed listening to ourselves offstage for the first time, and we played the tape of that show almost every night of the tour afterward. In a sense we became our own influence, which has never happened before.

THE "GHOST" played in Denver, like the Hamburg "Wolfman's Brother," displayed a richly textured, state-of-the-art Phish. "Ghost" is another perfect Phish jam vehicle that announces its own anything-goes status. In the same way that "Tweezer"'s freezer is full of surprises, each "Ghost" differs from all others from the moment the band finishes singing "I feel I've never told you the story of the ghost" for the final time.

The Denver "Ghost" story begins with a languorous groove the band settles into like it would a La-Z-Boy on the control deck of the mother ship. After that, the "Ghost" intensifies like the Hamburg "Wolfman's Brother" extended into another dimension. Phish stretches and contorts itself like a funky rubber band for minutes of intense rhythmic converse until Anastasio kicks on his digital delay over McConnell's looping synthesizer, and a cycling siren slightly out of phase with the band's interlocking gears hovers above the fray, a Frippish loop that keeps the groove keen, tense, and wary. When McConnell begins to concentrate on his grand piano, the cyclic carousel becomes less "funky" and more American, less African and more cyber, until it hits a hot rock peak and slowly subsides from turbulent volcanic intensity to buttery Lava-lamp mellow.

Aside from the dissonant and fiery spin art of "Down with Disease," the show's other apex consisted of a long, slow, jam coming out of Chuck Berry's "Johnny B. Goode" that combined classic eurotechno rhythms with pixilated melodies bringing to mind mercury raindrops on a hot tin roof.

Trey: Tom Marshall played drums and I played guitar on the demo version of "Ghost." We just started jamming without lyrics and spontaneously stopped a few minutes later. I rewound the tape, grabbed the mike, pushed record, and Tom handed me a poem to sing. As I got to the last line, the music we'd just recorded ended as though we'd planned it to, and you can hear the two of us falling to the ground screaming. The song wrote itself in about five minutes, and it catalyzed the entire fall tour.

Tom: In grade school and high school I was pretty sure I'd tapped into some kind of spiritual something I just called my "spirit." I really would talk to it and ask it for things, much like someone might pray to God. It definitely answered me in actions rather than words. It helped me through various teen traumas: friend or girl problems, school problems, and the like. But here's the weird part: My friend Phil housed my spirit. He knew it and alluded to it, but would never admit it outright. Sometimes when we were stoned together he would say strange things to me I construed as "proof" that he was my spirit. When I asked him directly about the spirit, he would only reply

OPPOSITE: The Phish crew, Fleet Center, December 30, 1996
ABOVE: Post–New Year's Eve: Trey and Phish road manager Brad Sands, Madison Square Garden, New York, New York, December 31, 1997

"Don't worry about it" or "I can't tell you more about that now." He often hinted that the answer would eventually be revealed, but it never was.

Phil and I were very close—maybe too close. As close as heterosexual male friends can be, I think. He left town right after high school and took my spirit with him. We parted ways almost completely—not even communicating much. I've asked him what he thought about the whole thing a few times since then, but he just shrugged the question off. When I asked him if he really was my spirit, he said he thinks we were just really good pals. Whatever. I'm pretty sure my spirit is still around. I just haven't found out who it's housed in at the moment. "Ghost" was my way of explaining the whole thing to Trey.

Page: If I ever felt as good about a studio album we recorded as I felt about that Denver show, I'd really feel I'd accomplished something. I was extremely proud of those first four fall tour shows. After thirteen years of playing together, we were making music I'd never heard before. I'd like to make an album where I felt exactly the same way.

Trey: I'd never heard anything quite like it before. We had this really cool thing going where my delay loops were out of sync with Fish's groove. Fish was laying down these heavy fat grooves, and filling in a lot fewer holes, which allowed Mike to come forward. 'Ninety-seven, after all, was the year of Mike, who came into his own. All of a sudden everybody started telling me, "I've never been able to hear the bass before, but now I can, and it's great." I don't think it has much to do with his bass sound, however. It has more to do with how he's playing, and it always has. The band created more space, he started playing more sparsely, and every note has a chance to develop in a huge room when he's playing more sparsely. It was no mystery to me.

Phish's top-heaviness disappeared as soon as we discovered our new rhythmic bed. I wasn't dragging the jams along anymore. Fish and Mike were carrying the jam while Page and I decorated the top. My delay loops combined with Page's cycling synthesizer lines began to create an intricate cross-hatching against Mike and Fish's more solid grooves.

Mike: On our nights off we'd go out to bars until two in the morning, drag a bunch of people back to the bus with us, and crank up the Denver show really loud. I'd never heard us sound anything like that; the bass and drums were so punchy. We'd bring in strobe lights and everybody would dance in the aisle.

Trey: In Worcester we played a sixty-minute-long "Runaway Jim" jam. When I listened to it afterward, it sounded as though we were in our living room, just jamming with no concern whatsoever for entertaining people. The concept of playing well or poorly never crossed my mind, it was just playing. What you get when you go down that road is oscillations back and forth between cringe-worthy moments of directionless plodding followed by five minutes of really amazing stuff. And that's what you get when you let go.

Fish: Screw-ups have now become opportunities for something cool and new to happen. Practically every excursion we've gone on for more than half an hour has started with somebody making a mistake. In 1995 or '96 I could sense a general panic whenever we felt nothing was happening in a jam and we felt obliged to *make* something happen. But in '97 we could just sit there, not thrash about, and know something would float to the surface.

Madison Square Garden, December 30, 1997

We've been in this band fourteen years, and half an hour between sets won't stop us from making the same mistakes: I speed up, Mike slows down, Trey counts off too fast. Everyone still has the same good and bad habits.

Trey: There were only two sets the whole tour that I didn't like. The first set the second night at Albany and one of the sets in Champaign, Illinois.

"GIMLET DREAMED THAT

A BRAND-NEW START OF IT: NEW YEAR'S EVE '97

NEWLY UNDER the influence of themselves, Phish took two weeks off before beginning their traditional four-night New Year's Eve run with a single show in Landover, Maryland, and then returned north for three nights at Madison Square Garden that would culminate in their latest New Year's Eve extravaganza. For the first time in years, the band removed itself from the stunt entirely. Neither did they plan anything so musically formidable as the previous year's divertissement, "Bohemian Rhapsody."

Nevertheless, the first thing the nineteen thousand ticket holders saw upon entering the venue was a white "egg," sixty feet in diameter, completely covering the Garden's overhead scoreboard. This egg served as a screen upon which four projectors cast the undulating images of lactating udder balls, olive-loaf piggies, Swiss cheese, fried eggs, porterhouse steaks, and lightbulbs during the course of the evening. The meat-and-dairy imagery was designed by Lars Fisk, whose outsized notions had festooned the Clifford Ball and the Great Went. The images served as intermittent teasers for the midnight extravaganza to come.

At ten minutes to midnight, while the band vamped funkily through "Also Sprach Zarathustra," a colorfully absurdist and sexy take on Darwinian evolution exploded onto the egg screen. Time's quickening pace was marked sporadically by a crazy little Biometer as the characters that had appeared during the previous two sets of music took their rightful place in evolutionary history. A humanoid suddenly appeared out of this condensation of creation only to morph immediately into the Statue of Liberty, which receded to reveal the New York skyline amid a swarm of animated characters whose whirling temporal implosion caused the egg screen to split open and drop huge balloon versions of the creatures.

This cosmic fertility ritual resonated nicely with the autobiographical foreshadowing Anastasio had improvised in the middle of the previous evening's "Harpua." "Somebody asked me if the 'Harpua' story was true," says Anastasio's father, Ernie, of his son's story involving the *Lost in Space* TV show, purloined family meals, and a schoolyard pentagram. "I said it happened in Trey's head the same way lots of things happen there. Which is to say every element of the story was true except one: We never ate steak."

Madison Square Garden, December 31, 1997: The egg cracks at midnight.

PHISH

Beauty
and Terror
meet in your
seat...as every
thrill of the story
comes off the screen
right at you in
NATURAL VISION
3-DIMENSION

THE EVE OF THE NEW YEAR
NINETEEN NINETY EIGHT
MADISON SQUARE GARDEN
NEW YORK   NEW YORK!

UNIQUE...!
THRILLING!
STARTLING!

Page: Over the past few years we've tried to become less involved in planning the New Year's stunts. As much as we want it to be good, and want to be a part of it, we don't want to have to spend the time or energy thinking about it. Certainly at the time it's happening, we shouldn't be thinking about it. We should be thinking about the music. Up until that point, it's just a pain in the ass and a huge bunch of decisions to be made. This one ended up being pretty expensive relative to how other ones have been. They're all pretty expensive when you get right down to it. Projecting things onto a screen has been done so much. Dropping balloons has been done so much too. The thing we always say when we start talking about New Year's projects is, "At least people got to see us fly in a hot dog." And you couldn't say that about this year. "At least we dropped a balloon" or "At least we projected something on a screen."

Trey: The '96 New Year's show was overly planned and safe, yet fun. The '97 show, on the other hand, was just a big blur to me. Our guest list was something like fifteen hundred people, and I felt completely at home during the three Madison Square Garden shows, completely comfortable. They were just three more gigs in the big picture. Nothing was planned. We just went onstage and jammed. In a certain sense the New Year's Eve show was actually the best example of what the whole year was, in the same way that '96's New Year's Eve show was the best example of what that year was.

Page: Musically we played pretty well for a New Year's Eve show. And "New York, New York" was a personal triumph. We didn't decide I was going to sing it until that afternoon. Somebody bought the CD that day, and I learned it between the first and second sets and taught it to the band between the second and third sets. Then we played it for the encore. Someone gave me a tape, and it was our outgoing message for a while.

Trey: We should open every New Year's Eve show leading up to the millennium with "2001," and play it longer and longer until it's the entire show in the year 2000.

Page: We're still an underground band, in a sense, because we're neither on MTV nor the radio.

We're somewhere on the fringe of popular culture where a lot of people have heard of us, a lot more haven't, and I suspect our popularity will rise and fall as the years go by. The Dead were always known as a live band, and perhaps that will be our legacy as well. They had an enormous cultural effect in spite of that and, strangely enough, ended up being one of the more influential bands of the eighties. And who would have predicted that?

Trey: All the strange things we've done—developing rehearsal exercises, analyzing ourselves, telling ourselves we're not allowed to analyze ourselves, not playing in this country for eight months, canning our song list and then bringing it back a month later—all those things are directed toward the same end, which is creating an onstage atmosphere in which we can play like ourselves and make a type of music that's completely unknown until the four of us get together, that in order to work has to by definition be totally different than any other music that's ever been. We want every show to feel like the first time we've ever played together, and in a sense it is. It seems like such a simple thing, but it's not. As Miles Davis said, sounding like yourself is the hardest thing to do, especially inside a group. That's the one other dimension—sounding like yourself in the context of a group. I don't know what I sound like, but I'm starting to know what I sound like with these three guys.

Page: A handful of bands out there have been or will be influenced by us in the live department. These bands see us as an example of a group that's just a bunch of guys that got together and were able to create live music that people really wanted to go see. And that's a great mark to leave. A lot could happen in the next few years. Phish might take off in ways I couldn't imagine, it may hover about as big as it is now, or dip down. A lot hinges on our next album, which might well turn out to be the sort of all-out rock record we've never tried to make before.

Trey: Sometimes it all gets crazy and we talk about taking a year off. We had a long, funny conversation about not doing a New Year's run in 1997. If we hadn't done it, we would have had a four-month block of time to write new music, rehearse, whatever. We argued about it for a good half-hour in the Dionysian conference room. Then there was a pause, and somebody said, "So what are we gonna do on New Year's Eve? Go to a party?" Everybody broke up laughing, and we booked Madison Square Garden.

Post–New Year's
Eve, 1997:
(LEFT TO RIGHT)
Trey, the Phish
organization's
Cynthia Brown,
the Dude of Life,
John Paluska,
and Jon Siket (in
background)
BELOW LEFT AND
FOLLOWING PAGES:
Madison Square
Garden, December
31, 1997

PERMISSION ACKNOWLEDGMENTS AND PHOTO/ILLUSTRATION CREDITS

PHOTO CREDITS

POSTER/ILLUSTRATION CREDITS